PROGRAMMER'S RESOURCE SERIES

Database Development

Eugene Eric Kim, editor

Bulldog Books
Miller Freeman Inc.
411 Borel Ave.
San Mateo, CA 94402

Programmer's Resource Series: Database Development
Eugene Eric Kim, editor

Cover design: *R. Bruce Gardner*
Design and production: *Jeff Brandenburg/ImageComp*

ISBN: 0-87930-480-4

Table of Contents

Preface

The Programmer's Resource Series is a joint effort of the leading magazines in the software-development arena—*Dr. Dobb's Journal*, *Dr. Dobb's Sourcebook*, *C/C++ Users Journal*, *Web Techniques*, *Windows Developer Journal*, and *Microsoft Systems Journal*. The contents of *Database Development* and other books in this series consists of relevant articles from the participating magazines. Thanks to the following individuals who made this book possible: Jonathan Erickson, Martha Masinton, Marc Briand, Ann Brocker, Michael Floyd, Eugene Eric Kim, Stan Barnes, and Peter Hutchinson. Most importantly, thanks to the author/programmers who shared their expertise and source code in the first place.

Introduction

Eugene Eric Kim

Computers have revolutionized our ability to process information, and yet, our fundamental techniques for managing data predate the modern computer. It is not entirely surprising, then, that although computer hardware has vastly improved, many important topics of the past are still relevant today.

As a result, a vast number of articles on databases—from the highly academic and technical to the management-oriented—continue to be published every year. Despite the maturity of the topic, we continue to see innovative and interesting developments in the database industry, and each new development gives birth to its own new and complex issues.

The introduction of relational databases in 1970 and SQL in 1974 shifted the focus from computational techniques for storing and retrieving data to the age old problem of information management. Most developers now focus mainly on designing database schema and integrating databases into applications.

Despite the increased standardization of database access via technologies such as SQL and ODBC, each different database-management system continues to contain its own unique nuances and thus, its own separate learning curve. Additionally, expanding traditionally C APIs to encompass other languages such as C++, Perl, and more recently, Java require a greater expertise of both the database management system and each language's personality.

Most of the authors in *Database Development* focus on the technical issues regarding use of these database-management systems. Erin Carroll and Andrew Wilson, for example, examine JDBC, an ODBC-like interface for accessing databases from Java, while Jeremy Woo-Sam and Tony Murphy discuss encapsulating the Oracle database's C API in C++. Greg Johnson shows how to access Binary Large OBject (BLOB) fields using the Microsoft Foundation Classes (MFC).

We move from these language-specific discussions to more general but no less detailed articles on ODBC and its core, the Call Level Interface (CLI). Roger Sippl describes the origins of CLI and closely analyzes this standard. Later, Alex Ragen gives a step-by-step account of programming a database using Microsoft's ODBC C API. Finally, Ken North examines API—as opposed to application—performance issues and introduces his APIBench application that benchmarks the performance of various APIs.

The World Wide Web has taken the entire computer industry by storm, and the database industry is no exception. The Web seems ideal as a universal interface to all sorts of information. However, there are some fundamental difficulties with developing Web database client applications. Ken North discusses some of these issues in his article on Web database programming.

The Web is also an ideal, worldwide platform for distributing objects, and hence, has heightened interest in another rapidly growing industry: object databases. The object database is a significant technology that is rapidly growing in popularity and yet woefully lacking in documentation. Unlike their relational cousins, there are no widely adopted standards for object databases. Simply grasping object technology is a complex task, and implementing it with the dearth of good documentation—especially in environments where legacy databases rule—have proven to be a great challenge.

A common and difficult problem with object databases is mapping an object's attribute to a relational model. Chuck Allison tackles one aspect of this problem by using C++ to store objects in a relational database table.

While most of the chapters in *Database Development* deal with integrating applications with databases, we cannot ignore the challenge of implementing and improving the database system itself. With this in mind, Pete Rail tells us how to develop a database cache manager using MFC.

Finally, Robert Krten reminds us that databases are pervasive in almost every kind of application and that an industrial-strength database is neither necessary nor necessarily suitable for all applications. Robert implements an indexed text-retrieval system using a database that comes free with every operating system—the file system.

The diversity and technical depth of the topics covered in *Database Development* clearly reflects the breadth and complexity of database development as well as the remarkable work developers like yourself continue to do in this field.

SQL Access Group's Call-Level Interface

Roger Sippl

The SQL Access Group (SAG) was formed in 1989 to define and promote standards for database portability and interoperability. Initially, the membership roster included database heavyweights Oracle, Informix, and Ingres (now Computer Associates), as well as hardware vendors Digital, Hewlett-Packard, Tandem, and Sun. Table 1 lists the current membership roster. The group's initial projects involved developing the draft ISO/ANSI standard for SQL (including the embedded-SQL interface specifications) and a specification for remote data access (RDA).

In 1990, SAG took the lead in developing an SQL-based Call Level Interface (CLI). The CLI SAG is an API for database access, offering an alternative invocation technique to embedded SQL that provides essentially equivalent operations. SAG envisioned an interface that would enable client/server applications

Roger is chairman of the SQL Access Group and founder of Visigenic Software. He can be contacted at Visigenic Software, 951 Mariner's Island Blvd., Suite 460, San Mateo, CA 94404, (415) 286-1900. *Reprinted courtesy of* Dr. Dobb's Sourcebook.

to access data stored in heterogeneous relational and nonrelational databases. The interface would be platform, vendor, database, and language neutral. SAG and X/Open published the CLI Snapshot Specification in 1992 as a "work in progress," and it was adopted for use in commercial software products.

Microsoft helped define the X/Open CLI specification and became the first company to commercialize the CLI specification by shipping Open Database Connectivity (ODBC) 1.0 for Windows in 1992. To create ODBC, Microsoft extended the CLI specification and created a three-layer specification in which the "core" layer corresponds to the SAG CLI. Over the next two years, the CLI specification underwent several transformations, reemerging in 1994 as an X/Open Preliminary Specification. Also in 1994, Microsoft released ODBC 2.0, whose core functionality was still aligned with the SAG CLI. Earlier this year, Microsoft announced that ODBC 3.0 (to be released in 1996) will be fully aligned with both ISO's CLI standard and SAG's CLI Specification.

In March 1995, the CLI was finalized and published as an X/Open Common Application Environment (CAE) specification. CAE specifications are adopted by consensus and are the basis against which suppliers brand their products. The adoption and publication of the CLI as an X/Open CAE specification represents the culmination of five years of cooperative development work within the SQL Access Group.

In the meantime, ODBC has gained broad support in the database industry. All major software vendors—Oracle, Sybase, Informix, Computer Associates, IBM, Gupta, Powersoft, and Borland, as well as more than 140 application-software developers and VARs—have added ODBC support. Many of these vendors also offer proprietary APIs; nonetheless, they see the X/Open CLI specification and ODBC as important to their strategy. In 1994, Microsoft granted an exclusive source-code license to Visigenic Software for porting and licensing the ODBC SDK to non-Windows platforms. As a result, the ODBC SDK is now also available on all major UNIX platforms, as well as OS/2 and Macintosh.

A Closer Look at the SAG CLI

The X/Open CLI specification is a standard API for database access that is vendor, platform, and database neutral. It defines a set of functions that a program can call directly using normal function-call facilities. The specification is language independent and includes header files for both C and Cobol.

The CLI specification defines 57 functions that support a rich set of database-access operations sufficient for creating robust database applications, including:

- Allocating and deallocating handles (eight calls).
- Getting and setting attributes (ten calls).
- Opening and closing database connections (two calls).
- Accessing descriptors (six calls).

- Executing SQL statements (nine calls).
- Retrieving results (eight calls).
- Accessing schema metadata (four calls).
- Performing introspection (four calls).
- Controlling transactions (two calls).
- Accessing diagnostic information (three calls).
- Canceling functions (one call).

A database application calls these functions for all interactions with a database. The CLI enables applications to establish multiple database connections simultaneously and to process multiple statements simultaneously, depending on the capabilities of the database servers being accessed. Figures 1 and 2 show the basic control flow for using the CLI functions.

The X/Open CLI specification was developed with client/server architectures in mind. In fact, the CLI is ideal for this environment, in which the developer often knows little (if anything) about the database at the time the application is written. The X/Open CLI specification defines a set of introspection functions that enable an application to discover the characteristics and capabilities of a particular CLI implementation and of any database server accessed through that implementation. For example, *SQLGetTypeInfo* lets you find out what data types are supported by a particular server, and *SQLDataSources* returns a list of available database servers and descriptions. Introspection functions facilitate a technique known as "adaptive programming," whereby an application adapts its behavior at run time to take advantage of the capabilities of a particular database environment.

AT&T
Borland International
Computer Associates
Fulcrum Technologies
Hitachi
IBM
Information Builders
Informix Software
INTERSOLV
Microsoft
Oracle
Progress Software
Sybase
Visigenic Software

Table 1: *SQL Access Group members.*

Processing SQL Statements

The X/Open CLI specification, including sample programs and header files, is available directly from X/Open. Listings One, Two, and Three illustrate how the CLI works. Listing One is from a typical database application. Listings Two and Three are the significant portions of functions called by Listing One.

The application allocates memory for an environment handle and a connection handle; both are required to establish a database connection. The *SQLConnect* call establishes the database connection, specifying the server name (*server_name*), user id (*uid*), and password (*pwd*). The application then allocates memory for a

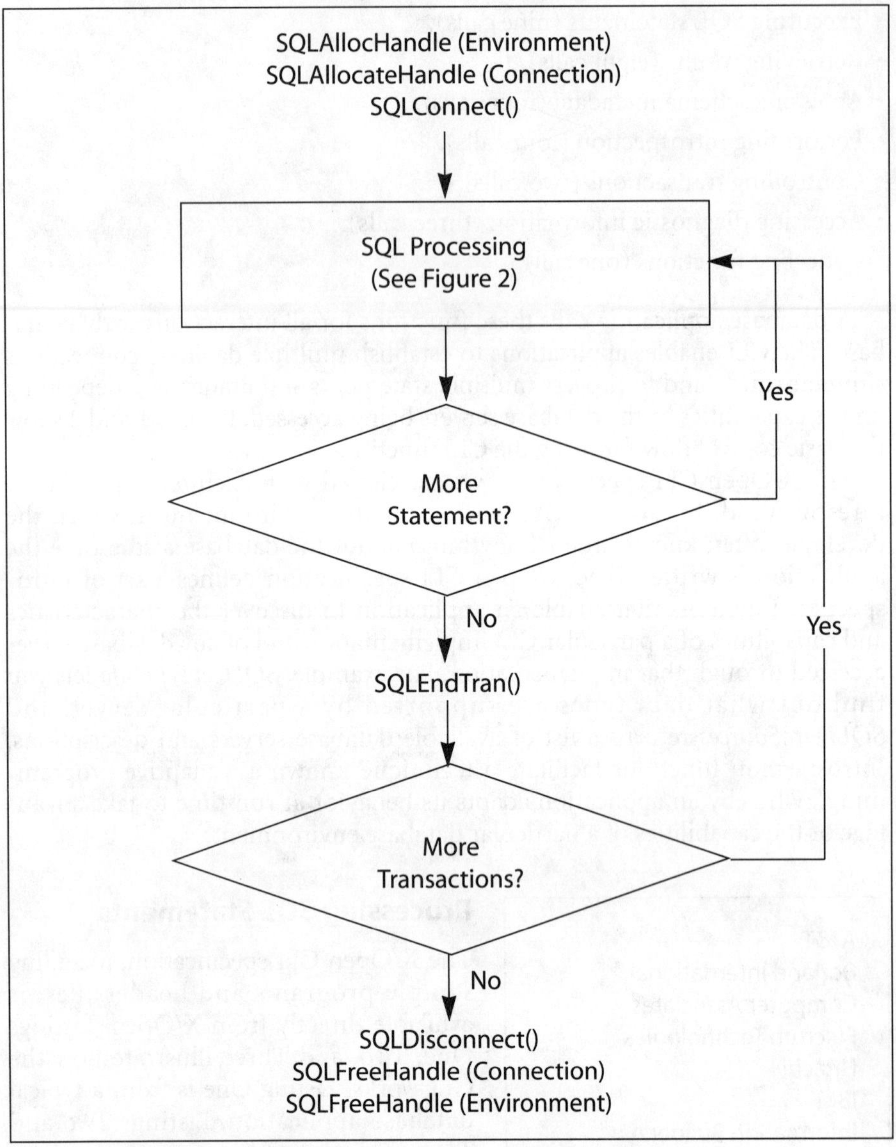

Figure 1: *Basic CLI control flow.*

statement handle and calls *SQLExecDirect*, which both prepares and executes an SQL statement. The *SQLGetDiagField* call takes advantage of the CLI's ability to interrogate the database server. In this case, it returns a code describing the nature of the SQL statement just executed. With this information in hand, the application calls the user-defined *DoSelect()* function to process the results of the SQL statement. Finally, the program frees the statement handle, disconnects from the database, and frees the memory previously allocated for the connection and environment handles.

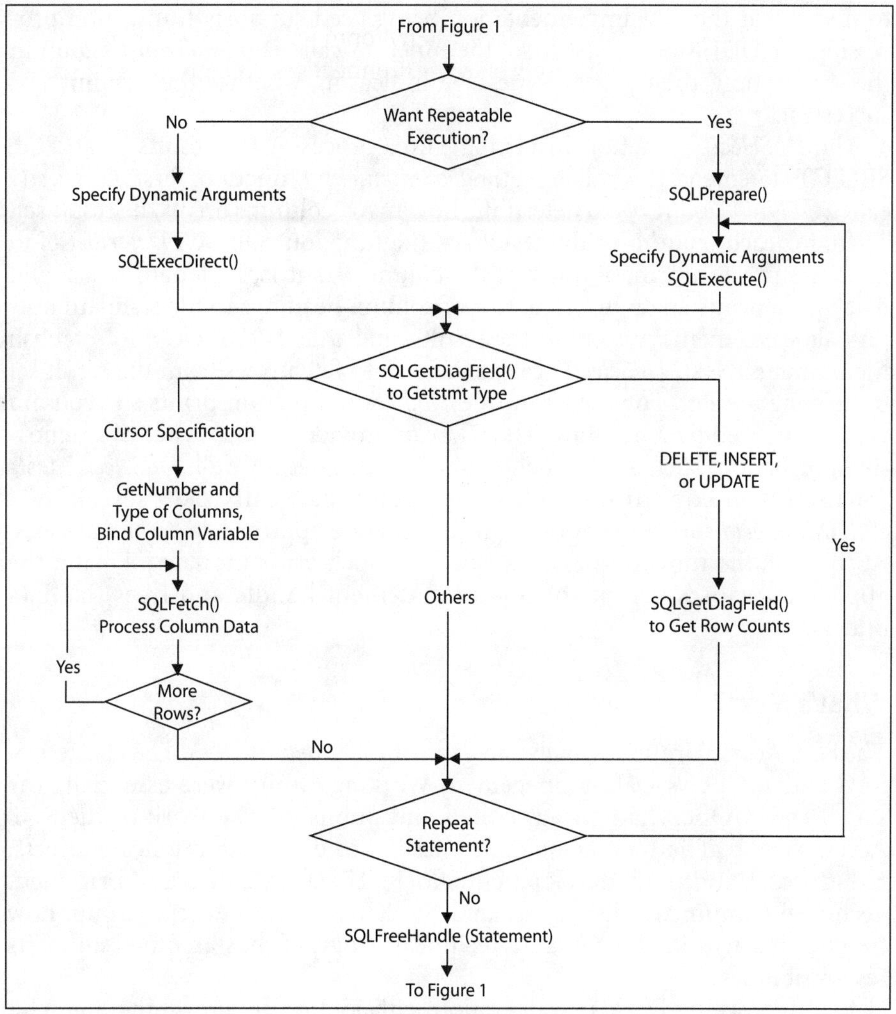

Figure 2: ***CLI control flow for processing SQL statements.***

The body of the *DoStatement()* function in Listing Two is built around a switch statement that processes the results of an SQL statement based on the return value from the *SQLGetDiagField* call in Listing One. In the case of a SELECT statement, which requires its own complex processing, the function calls another user-defined function, *DoSelect()*; see Listing Three. In the case of an UPDATE, DELETE, or INSERT statement, the *DoStatement()* function calls the CLI diagnostic function *SQLGetDiagField* to find out how many rows were affected by the statement, then calls *SQLEndTran* to commit the transaction. The function prints one message indicating whether the commit was successful and another giving the number of affected rows.

In the case of any Data Definition Language (DDL) statement, the *DoStatement()* function first calls the CLI introspection function *SQLGetInfo* to find out if the CLI implementation being used supports transaction processing for DDL statements. If so, the function calls *SQLEndTran* to commit the transaction, then prints a message indicating whether the commit was successful.

The *DoSelect()* function in Listing Three processes the results of an SQL SELECT statement. It is called by the *DoStatement()* function. First, *DoSelect()* calls *SQLNumResultCols* to determine how many columns are in the result set. Then, for each column in the result set, the function calls *SQLDescribeCol* to get descriptive information about the column (that is, its length, scale, and data type), prints an appropriate row of column headings to the standard output, allocates memory to bind the results, and calls *SQLBindCol* to establish the bindings. Next, *DoSelect()* calls *SQLFetch* to fetch rows from the result set until none are left. For each row, the *DoSelect()* function prints the column values, followed by a new line. The CLI can provide various types of diagnostic information, such as whether a value is truncated or null; *DoSelect()* tests for these two conditions and, when they occur, calls the user-defined *BuildMessage()* function (not shown) to generate appropriate error messages. At the end, the function prints a list of any such error messages. Finally, the application closes the cursor for the statement handle and frees the data buffers.

What's Next?

The SQL Access Group formally merged with X/Open in 1995. The charters of SAG and X/Open's Data Management Working Group were essentially the same, and X/Open had always edited and published the work of the SQL Access Group. The merger made it possible to eliminate duplicate efforts, reduce costs, and unify development efforts. The X/Open Data Management Technical Committee disbanded, and the X/Open SQL Access Group, now functioning within the X/Open Technical Program, has assumed all of its responsibilities.

SAG is working in close cooperation with ISO on its upcoming SQL CLI specification, which is intended to mirror the X/Open specification. SAG is also actively pursuing the next logical step for the CLI—the development of an X/Open test suite for CLI conformance. Such a test suite will enable developers to verify conformance to the CLI Specification. Development of the test suite should be well underway by the time this article is published.

SAG has already begun work on the next version of the CLI specification. Our mission is to extend and refine the CLI for even more successful interoperability and to define standards that incorporate newer database technologies, including XA transaction processing, stored procedures, BLOBs, triggers, and asynchronous calls.

The efforts of the major standards organizations, including ISO, ANSI, and X/Open, as well as the strategies of all the major players in the database industry, now incorporate the X/Open CLI Specification. Vendors and standards organizations are moving rapidly in the same direction, a direction the marketplace has already validated.

Listing One

```
/* allocate an environment handle */
SQLAllocHandle(SQL_HANDLE_ENV, SQL_NULL_HANDLE, &henv);

/* allocate a connection handle */
SQLAllocHandle(SQL_HANDLE_DBC, henv, &hdbc);

/* connect to database */
if (SQLConnect(hdbc, server_name, SQL_NTS, uid, SQL_NTS, pwd, SQL_NTS) !=
        SQL_SUCCESS)
    return(PrintErr(SQL_HANDLE_DBC, hdbc));

/* allocate a statement handle */
SQLAllocHandle(SQL_HANDLE_STMT, hdbc, &hstmt);

/* execute the SQL statement */
if (SQLExecDirect(hstmt, sqlstr, SQL_NTS) != SQL_SUCCESS)
    return(PrintErr(SQL_HANDLE_STMT, hstmt));

/* see what kind of statement it was */
SQLGetDiagField(SQL_HANDLE_STMT, hstmt, 0, SQL_DIAG_DYNAMIC_FUNCTION_CODE,
       (SQLPOINTER)&stmttype, 0, (SQLSMALLINT *)NULL);

/* process the SQL statement */
DoStatement(stmttype);

/* free statement handle */
SQLFreeHandle(SQL_HANDLE_STMT, hstmt);

/* disconnect from database */
SQLDisconnect(hdbc);

/* free connection handle */
SQLFreeHandle(SQL_HANDLE_DBC, hdbc);

/* free environment handle */
SQLFreeHandle(SQL_HANDLE_ENV, henv);
```

Listing Two

```
switch(stmttype) {
    /* SELECT statement */
    case SQL_DIAG_SELECT_CURSOR:
        DoSelect();
        break;
    /* searched UPDATE, searched DELETE, or INSERT statement */
    case SQL_DIAG_UPDATE_WHERE:
    case SQL_DIAG_DELETE_WHERE:
    case SQL_DIAG_INSERT:
```

```
        /* get row count */
        SQLGetDiagField(SQL_HANDLE_STMT, hstmt, 0, SQL_DIAG_ROW_COUNT,
            (SQL_POINTER)&rowcount, 0, (SQLSMALLINT *)NULL);
        if (SQLEndTran(SQL_HANDLE_ENV, henv, SQL_COMMIT) == SQL_SUCCESS)
            printf("Operation successful\n");
        else
            printf("Operation failed\n");
        printf("%ld rows affected\n", rowcount);
        break;
    /* other statements */
    case SQL_DIAG_ALTER_TABLE:
    case SQL_DIAG_CREATE_INDEX:
    case SQL_DIAG_CREATE_TABLE:
    case SQL_DIAG_CREATE_VIEW:
    case SQL_DIAG_DROP_INDEX:
    case SQL_DIAG_DROP_TABLE:
    case SQL_DIAG_DROP_VIEW:
    case SQL_DIAG_GRANT:
    case SQL_DIAG_REVOKE:
        SQLGetInfo(hdbc, SQL_TXN_CAPABLE, &txn_type, 0, 0);
        if(txn_type == SQL_TC_ALL) {
            if (SQLEndTran(SQL_HANDLE_ENV, henv, SQL_COMMIT) ==
                    SQL_SUCCESS)
                printf("Operation successful\n");
            else
                printf("Operation failed\n");
        }
        break;
    /* other implementation-defined statements */
    default:
        printf("Statement type=%ld\n", stmttype);
        break;
}
```

Listing Three

```
/* determine number of result columns */
SQLNumResultCols(hstmt, &nresultcols);

/* display column names */
for (i=0; i<nresultcols; i++) {
    SQLDescribeCol(hstmt, i+1, colname, sizeof(colname), &colnamelen,
            &coltype, collen[i], &scale, &nullable);
    /* user-defined function to get the display length for the data type */
    collen[i] = DisplayLength(coltype, collen[i], colname);
    printf("%*.*s", collen[i], collen[i], colname);
    /* allocate memory to bind column */
    data[i] = (SQLCHAR *) malloc(collen[i]+1);
    /* bind columns to program vars, converting all types to CHAR */
    SQLBindCol(hstmt, i+1, SQL_CHAR, data[i], collen[i]+1, &outlen[i]);
}
printf("\n");

/*display result rows */
```

```
while (SQL_SUCCEEDED(rc=SQLFetch(hstmt))) {
    errmsg[0] = '\0';
    for (i=0; i<nresultcols; i++)  {
        if (outlen[i] == SQL_NULL_DATA || outlen[i] >= collen[i])
            /* set data text to "NULL" or add to errmsg */
            BuildMessage(errmsg, (SQLPOINTER *)&data[i], collen[i],
                    &outlen[i], i);
        printf("%*,*s ", outlen[i], outlen[i], data[i]);
    } /* for all columns in this row */
    /* print any accumulated error messages and new line */
    printf("%s\n", errmsg);
} /* while rows to fetch */

SQLCloseCursor(hstmt);
/* free data buffers */
for (i=0; i<nresultcols; i++) {
    free(data[i]);
}
```

End Listings

C Database Programming with ODBC

Alex Ragen

I make a living by writing applications that acquire and present data in useful forms, so I'm always looking for tools that help me organize and present data. These days, a number of powerful database packages are available — such as Microsoft Access or Borland Paradox — that provide not only credible database engines, but all kinds of nearly spectacular tools for designing forms and reports as well. Using these packages would greatly shorten development time for me, but I have avoided them because they all suffer one crippling limitations: they are set up to receive input data only from a user typing at a keyboard.

These applications do have provisions for importing data from ASCII files, and even other applications, but these imports are expected to occur on a one-

Alex Ragen is a consultant based in Jerusalem, Israel. You can reach him at Alex@CheckPoint.com.
Reprinted courtesy of C/C++ Users Journal.

time basis, usually when setting the system up for the first time. For me, this limitation is a serious one, because in the systems I design, most of the data originates elsewhere: an instrument directly attached to the computer or a device communicating over a telephone line. It's difficult and sometimes impossible to do this kind of data acquisition with these database packages.

These packages typically provide limited programming support by offering a native variant of Basic, or some similar language. For a dyed-in-the-wool C programmer like me, this "support" amounts to a restriction. Still, I have watched with envy as other developers whipped out very sophisticated systems in a matter of weeks using database packages, and I've tried to find ways to use them myself.

Recently, I've succeeded in building two applications that combine the best of both worlds — a convenient and easy-to-use database with good old C — without sacrificing any flexibility. The secret: an old-new standard for maintaining databases called ODBC (Open Data Base Connectivity). If this sounds

What is SQL

SQL stands for "Structured Query Language." SQL started out as the query language for the System/R project at IBM's Santa Teresa laboratories in the mid-1970s. System/R was a project that grew out of Ted Codd's pioneering work on relational databases and was the forerunner of DB2. A relational database is a database organized around the table model, where rows correspond to what are commonly called records and columns correspond to fields. The logical model of a relational database is of a collection of tables, with no pointers — only key values. The database engine maintains pointers, to be sure, but these pointers are hidden from the developer. Having no explicit pointers and having an ability to dynamically modify its own structure (new tables, rows and even columns can be added at any time) makes a relational database conceptually simple and very flexible.

SQL is a simple database manipulation language built around a small number of statements. `WHERE` introduces a condition, as in `WHERE Inventory < 30`. `SELECT` retrieves data, as in `SELECT MachineID FROM MACHINE` which retrieves all the values of the column `MachineID` from the table `MACHINE`. `UPDATE` updates data, as in `UPDATE MACHINE SET Capacity = 33 WHERE Inventory < 30` which sets the value of `Capacity` to `33` in all the rows of the table `MACHINE` where the value of `Inventory` is less than `30`. `DELETE` deletes data, as in `DELETE FROM MACHINE WHERE Inventory < 50`, which deletes from the table `MACHINE` all rows where the value of `Inventory` is less than `50`. In addition, SQL has statements to add or delete columns, to generate totals or sort rows, to join different tables to create a temporary table for query purposes, and to nest queries within queries. Most DBMSs include an interactive SQL processor, so that someone with no programming experiences can query and update a database. Of course, the DBMS also incorporates security safeguards to prevent the inexperienced and adventurous from having free reign of the company data.

The Growth of SQL

SQL's growth from a restricted query language to a full-scale database manipulation language has led to an explosive growth in the number of relational database engines.

too good to be true, I should add that I paid a price for this success, but in my case it was well worth it. After reading this article, you can judge for yourself whether this approach is useful to you, and whether you're willing to pay the price.

The database I used was Microsoft Access 2.0. I could just as well have used Paradox, or any other database for which ODBC drivers are available. I chose Access for rather mundane reasons; I had read some good reviews in the press and also, as a user of other components of Microsoft Office, I was able to get a good price on Access. In almost everything that follows, you can substitute Paradox or any other ODBC compliant database of your choice for Access.

If you've ever used something called "embedded SQL," then you already know what ODBC is like. (See the sidebar for more information about SQL.) When you want to perform some database activity in your C program — for example, if you want to query the database or update it — then you simply call a function and supply the appropriate SQL statement. From this short

All of these engines attempt strict adherance to the ever-evolving ANSI/ISO SQL standards, but some engines also differentiate themselves by adding proprietary "improvements." SQL's strengths (flexibility and conceptual simplicity) are the sources of its weaknesses: inflexibility and lack of speed. Pointers buried deep in the inaccessible database structure are unavailable to programmers, and often go unexploited. It is the database engine and not the programmer who decides on an access plan. SQL's stubborn insistence on seeing the world in terms of independent context-free rows and columns makes it difficult to fully take advantage of structures as repeating groups. Still, you can't argue with success. None of the major DBMS vendors have strayed from SQL, and it seems likely to remain with us in its various standard forms for some time to come. Oracle, Ingres, Access, Paradox, Sybase, SQL Server, SQLBase, and other SQL DBMS vendors overwhelmingly dominate the marketplace.

Making SQL More Accessible

Embedded SQL was an early attempt at making SQL accessible from other languages. The programmer would embed SQL statements in his program and a preprocessor would translate them into something the language compiler (usually Cobol but sometimes C) could handle. Embedded SQL is very highly vendor specific, since each vendor supplies different interface functions and no attempt at portability has been made.

Microsoft published the ODBC specification in 1992, ostensibly in response to the call of the SQL Access Group (a vendor group) for a call-level interface to SQL. In 1993 Apple and Microsoft agreed to support ODBC on Windows and Macintosh, in effect ensuring ODBC's status as the standard call-level SQL interface.

Learning SQL

Most DBMS vendors include an introduction to SQL in their documentation. These books are usually well suited to those who are already familiar with the subject. You can also try your local computer bookstore. I have used and like *The LAN TIMES Guide to SQL*, by James R. Groff and Paul N. Weinberg, Osborne McGraw-Hill, 1994 [3]. ❑

description of ODBC, you can infer two of its essential characteristics: it's designed for use with relational databases and you have to know SQL in order to use it. Whether you consider these characteristics strengths or shortcomings depends on your attitude toward relational databases in general.

Matters of philosophy aside, here's how I would go about constructing a mixed C-ODBC-Access application: First, build the database with Access. Forget about ODBC and C for the time being. One word of warning — you must plan your database very carefully. Resist the temptation to rush ahead and start designing forms and reports simply because they're so easy to churn out. Concentrate first and foremost on the design of the tables and the relationships between them, and run your design past your users. Once the database has been finalized, fill the tables with sample data, including the data that will, in the real system, come from non-keyboard sources. Generate some sample reports. Make sure the database is functioning as it is supposed to. Later on, when you add the ODBC components to your application, you'll want to be sure that the database component is functioning properly so that you'll be better able to isolate problems.

Using ODBC

The relevant components of ODBC are as follows:

- ODBC.INI
- ODBC.DLL
- individual ODBC drivers for each database

`ODBC.INI5` provides information about the databases that you will access with ODBC. The first section of the INI file is a list of all the databases and their types, for example:

```
[ODBC Data Sources]
MS Access Databases=Access Data (*.mdb)
MS Access 2.0 Databases=Access 2.0 for MS Office (*.mdb)
SuperApp=Access Data (*.mdb)
```

The above example indicates that three data sources are considered Microsoft Access databases: MS Access Databases, MS Access 2.0 Databases, and SuperApp. Each of the data sources listed in the ODBC Data Sources section is described in greater detail in a section of its own, later on in the file:

```
[SuperApp]
Driver=C:\WINDOWS\SYSTEM\ODBCJT16.DLL
DefaultDir=C:\SUPERAPP
JetIniPath=MSACC20.INI
DBQ=SUPERAPP.MDB
UID=Admin
Description= SuperApp Database
```

```
DataDirectory=c:\SUPERAPP\SUPERAPP.mdb
SingleUser=False
UseSystemDB=True
FileType=RedISAM
SystemDB=c:\SUPERAPP\system.mda
```

This example describes the SuperApp database as a Microsoft Access database whose ODBC driver is `C:\WINDOWS\SYSTEM\ODBCJT16.DLL`, and whose name is `SUPERAPP.MDB` in the directory `c:\SUPERAPP`.

To use a database with ODBC in a C program, you must do the following:

Initialize the ODBC environment

The `SQLAllocEnv` function allocates memory for an environment handle and initializes ODBC for an application:

```
return (SQLAllocEnv(&hEnv) == SQL_SUCCESS);
```

Connect to the database

The `SQLAllocConnect` function allocates a connection handle and the `SQLConnect` function actually makes the connection. ODBC looks up the database in `ODBC.INI` and then connects to it using the specified driver. If `SQLConnect` fails, it's usually a sign that something is wrong in `ODBC.INI` or that the required driver is missing.

```
if ((nResult = SQLAllocConnect(hEnv,(HDBC FAR *)&hDBC))
    != SQL_SUCCESS) {
    ... error message ...
}
nResult = SQLConnect(hDBC,(LPSTR)szDBName,SQL_NTS,
    (LPSTR)szUserName,SQL_NTS,
    (LPSTR)szPassword,SQL_NTS);
if (nResult != SQL_SUCCESS && nResult !=
    SQL_SUCCESS_WITH_INFO) {
    ... error message ...
}
```

Query/Update the Database

You query or update the database using SQL statements. For example, to update a database, you first allocate an SQL statement handle:

```
if ((nResult = SQLAllocStmt(hDBC,&hStatement))
    != SQL_SUCCESS) {
    ... error message ...
}
```

Then you build an SQL statement to do whatever it is you want to do. The following statement updates the `MACHINE` table, changing the values of the fields (columns in SQL jargon) `HardwareVersion`, `SoftwareVersion` in the record (row in SQL) whose MachineID field equals whatever is in szMachineID:

```
// ODBC SQL statement handle
HSTMT hStatement = SQL_NULL_HSTMT;
sprintf(pUpdate, "UPDATE DISTINCTROW MACHINE SET "
        " MACHINE.HardwareVersion = %d,"
        " MACHINE.SoftwareVersion = %d"
        " WHERE (\"MachineID\"=%s );",
        HardwareVersion,SoftwareVersion, szMachineID);
```

Then you execute the SQL statement

```
nResult = SQLExecDirect(hStatement, pUpdate, QL_NTS);
if (nResult != SQL_SUCCESS)
    ... error message ...
```

The following code fragment retrieves an unspecified number of records satisfying the given criteria from the EVENT table. Because EventID is the only field in the SELECT list, only EventID is available for later processing:

```
// ODBC SQL statement handle
HSTMT hStatement = SQL_NULL_HSTMT;
RETCODE nResult;
long lEventID;
sprintf(pSelect,"SELECT DISTINCTROW EventID "
        " FROM EVENT WHERE ((MachineID = %s) AND "
        " (Status = 0) AND (EventCode = %d));",
        pQTask->szMachineID, iNoPeriodicalReport);
        nResult = SQLExecDirect(hStatement,pSelect,
                                SQL_NTS);
if (nResult != SQL_SUCCESS) {
    DisplayError(nResult,hStatement);
    SQLFreeStmt(hStatement,SQL_DROP);
    return;
}
```

The next fragment binds the EventID field (the 0th field in the SELECT list) with the long variable lEventID:

```
nResult = SQLBindCol(hStatement,1,SQL_C_LONG,
                     &(lEventID), 0,NULL);
if (nResult != SQL_SUCCESS) {
DisplayError(nResult,hStatement);
SQLFreeStmt(hStatement,SQL_DROP);
return;
}
```

The following `while` statement (in C) loops through all the retrieved rows. Each time `SQLFetch` is successfully called, a new value appears in `lEventID`.

```
while (TRUE) {
    nResult = SQLFetch(hStatement);
    if (nResult != SQL_SUCCESS) { // no more rows
        break;
    }
    ... do something with lEventID ...
}
```

Free the SQL Statement Handle

When you're done querying or updating the database, you need to free the SQL statement handle:

```
SQLFreeStmt(hStatement,SQL_DROP);
```

Disconnect From the Database

The following C code disconnects from a database by breaking the connection established by `SQLConnect`:

```
SQLDisconnect(hDBC);
```

freeing the handle allocated by `SQLAllocConnect`:

```
SQLFreeConnect(hDBC);
```

and freeing the environment allocated by `SQLAllocEnv`

```
SQLFreeEnv(hEnv);
```

Debugging

It's best, in my experience, to isolate all the functions that call ODBC functions into a single source file. This file is then the only one that needs to include `sql.h` and `sqlext.h`. One of the sample applications in the ODBC SDK is `qurydemo`, which is a sort of generic query program. If I was having a problem with an Access query, I would have Access translate the offending query to SQL. Then I would copy the SQL text to the clipboard, paste it into `qurydemo`'s window and run the query. This process enabled me to isolate the problem more effectively than if I had tried to debug using Access's very limited debugging tools.

Getting it all Working

The techniques described here are the same for all databases. Presumably, if you decide to switch databases in mid-project, all you have to do is get hold of the appropriate ODBC driver and update `ODBC.INI`. You shouldn't even have to recompile your C code. That's the theory, anyway. In practice you may have to modify any of the SQL statements whose syntax is unique to the SQL dialect favored by your former database.

What I read about ODBC seemed pretty straightforward, and I didn't expect any problems when I started my projects, but of course I ran into a surprise or two along the way. I obtained the ODBC SDK from the Microsoft Developer's Network. The SDK includes drivers, example code, and lots of documentation on CD-ROM.

I also bought a print copy of Microsoft's ODBC 2.0 Programmers' Reference and SDK Guide and got to work. I discovered that the documentation was incomplete and oriented more to ODBC driver writers than to ODBC users. For example, the documentation for the `ODBC.INI` parameters is very sketchy. Until I came across (on CompuServe) an (apparent) Microsoft inter-office memo, I didn't know about the `DBQ` parameter and my application couldn't direct ODBC all the way to the database file, but only as far as the directory.

In the course of debugging, I got stuck on a problem and turned to CompuServe for help. My question "Can you advise me where I can get an up-to-date list of Jet [MS Access] database engine error messages?" produced the following reply from Microsoft: "If you are using the Access 2.0 ODBC driver then I would expect you to get all sorts of internal database errors from your program. The Access 2.0 ODBC driver that ships with Access 2.0 currently works only with MS Office products Excel and Word. We are currently working on the 2.0 ODBC driver to work with other products like VC++ but no release date has been given." By all rights the rest of this story should have been nothing but wail and woe, but it turned out to be just the opposite. I figured out the solution to my problem without Microsoft's help, and I have never had any of the internal database errors they promised me.

Is It Worth It?

On the upside, using Access and ODBC got me off to a quick start, and the user interface is one of the best I have ever done. If I had done it all in straight C, it would have taken me six months more, at the least, and the user interface wouldn't have been nearly as good. I gained a reliable, first-rate database and a quick-and-beautiful GUI. Best of all, I didn't have to give up my favorite language (after French). On the downside, ODBC and Access are both very slow. Relational databases have a well-deserved bad name when it comes to speed, and Access is definitely not an exception to the rule. My users haven't complained about speed yet — they're not programmers and don't know much about nanoseconds or clock cycles — and as time goes by they'll be running my systems on Pentiums or better, so speed won't be so important. However, if I were building a system where lightning speed was critical, I would steer clear of ODBC.

It is possible to speed things up by "preparing" a frequently executed SQL statement and then using `SQLExec` instead of `SQLExecDirect`. When using

SQLEXEC, the statement is parsed and an access plan prepared only once. However, if the underlying database is slow, or located somewhere over the network beyond a gateway, the speedup isn't likely to make much difference. In summary, I would definitely recommend considering the mixed C-ODBC-Access, but there are still some cases where the old ways are best.

Resources and References

[1] Microsoft Developers Network — This is a subscription service of Microsoft that provides technical articles, documentation, code, and utilities to Windows developers. Regular updates are issued on CD-ROM. Contact Microsoft Corp., One Microsoft Way, Redmond, VA 98053.

[2] *ODBC 2.0 Programmer's Reference and SDK Guide*, ISBN 155-615-6588 (Microsoft Press, 1995).

[3] James R. Groff and Paul N. Weinberg. *The LAN Times Guide to SQL* (Osborne McGraw-Hill, 1994).

Building Web Databases

Ken North

Web developers looking to SQL databases as a source for active content must consider that the users behind the browsers are engaged in disparate activities ranging from order processing to decision-support queries to time-series analysis. Furthermore, the model has changed: Client/server applications have a front and back end, while the common thread for Web projects is a browser front end, Web pages, HTML, and search engines. Although the methods for delivering content are similar, the "under-the-covers" data-access technologies may vary greatly because developers must tailor the database solution to the problem at hand. Some developers are putting up databases to permit World Wide Web users to search catalogs, shop for auto insurance, or order smoked fish. Others are marrying Web techniques with client/server SQL technology to provide workgroup, departmental, and enterprise databases. Factors such as parallel processing and commodity hardware are also driving the demand for access to data warehouses.

Programming database applications built with Web technology raises several technical issues. HTML, the language used to format most Web pages, doesn't easily support data-validation concepts such as required fields. The Hypertext Transfer Protocol (HTTP) used to present Web pages is stateless. An HTTP application typically connects, generates a `GET` request, and disconnects, whereas database applications often require persistent connections.

This article describes current approaches to data access and discusses the many tools available to database developers. It also presents a Java application

---

Ken is a consultant and independent software developer who writes and conducts seminars. He is the author of Windows Multi-DBMS Programming *(John Wiley & Sons).* *Reprinted courtesy of* Web Techniques.

that demonstrates how to get feature information for a DBMS or ODBC driver.

CGI, ISAPI, or NSAPI?

Many early solutions to Web data access relied on the Common Gateway Interface (CGI) and server-side helper applications. The disadvantage to CGI applications is that a Web server starts up an instance of the program for each user request. For database applications, this means the Web server forks or uses a process-per-database connection. Microsoft's Internet Information Server API (ISAPI) permits developers to write server applications that are analogous to CGI helper applications. However, ISAPI applications are implemented as dynamic link libraries (DLLs) so they don't use a process per request. The Internet Information Server uses a multithreaded architecture and maintains a pool of threads to service requests. Because ISAPI uses a DLL or shared library architecture, ISAPI applications must utilize thread-safe, reentrant code. The Netscape Server API (NSAPI) was also developed to get around CGI issues.

Other problems involve the nature of the back-end (database) processing. Transaction processing such as order-entry applications must be optimized to produce short-running queries for hundreds or thousands of concurrent users. A data-warehouse application, on the other hand, will have fewer users, but they will generate longer-running queries.

Persistent Connections and Query Accelerators

One of the issues for SQL applications is long-running queries. Web applications magnify design or optimization problems because many concurrent users can be affected by inefficient queries. SQL servers typically include an optimizer that determines the optimum access path for a query and provides feedback in the form of a query-execution plan to permit users to tune queries. Poorly designed SQL can tie up resources, so some companies market software governors that restrict queries to a predefined number of rows in the result set. Sites that marry a browser with data marts or data warehouses must place a premium on database design, query optimization, and tools such as query accelerators. Sybase's new IQ Server is a query accelerator that uses predefined joins and provides a variety of data-access techniques (not just B-tree indexing). IQ stores data by column rather than by row and does column-wise data compression. This means that rows can contain a variety of data types but columns will be of a similar makeup.

Transaction Processing

Transaction processing (TP) software and monitors are becoming more commonplace in client/server SQL applications. New products such as lightweight Transarc Encina clients and Microsoft Distributed Transaction Coordinator are likely to increase the number of applications built with transaction monitors. Transaction processing provides guarantees of completion and maintains data integrity by blocking invalid, partial updates. TP monitors or coordinators permit developers to manage transactions that might involve processes on multiple machines operating against heterogeneous databases and servers. Many companies have been doing this with dedicated hardware and networks, but transaction processing using an intranet architecture seems to be a growth industry.

Accessing SQL Databases

The spotlight on the Internet has motivated most SQL vendors and many other software companies to develop solutions for accessing SQL databases from Web applications. Some solutions provide links to databases using proprietary or SQL native APIs. Others rely on middleware such as Microsoft's Open Database Connectivity (ODBC) and Sun Microsystems' (JavaSoft) Java Database Connectivity (JDBC). ODBC and JDBC are both related to the X/Open SQL Call Level Interface (CLI), so they follow a common model. Applications use SQL queries for access to data and process answers in the form of query-result sets or diagnostic information.

ODBC is a multidatabase API that permits a single set of functions to operate on a variety of SQL databases. The ODBC architecture uses loadable database drivers that connect to multidatabase gateways or specific databases such as Sybase. ODBC gateways—commonly called ODBC servers—include the network and client libraries used to connect to a variety of SQL servers. Clients of the ODBC server use only a single driver to connect to a variety of data sources. JavaSoft's JDBC follows the single-API, multiple-database paradigm and, like ODBC, uses a driver manager to load drivers. JDBC operates at a higher level of abstraction than ODBC, so JDBC drivers don't implement the low-level functions seen in ODBC drivers.

Because performance and interoperability issues are magnified by the Web, developers using ODBC often reduce network traffic by caching connections, metadata, and other static information. Web products using ODBC need to follow that convention to minimize overhead when processing large numbers of requests. One reason to use a multidatabase API is to write applications or applets that can operate on heterogeneous SQL databases. To write interoperable code, a developer needs to use logic that determines at execution time the features and data types available for a database and its driver. ODBC and JDBC include support for metadata that permits a developer to use adaptive programming techniques.

DBMS vendors offer Web-server connections to their own databases while companies such as Working Set, Ensodex, Visigenic, and Intersolv offer servers that can connect to a variety of databases using ODBC, JDBC, or both. Oracle Web Server is a product that bundles SQL*Net and an Oracle Workgroup Server. It supports PL/SQL stored procedures, CGI 1.1, and HTML 2/3 tags. Sybase's web.sql product works with Sybase 11 servers running on Solaris, SGI

IRIX, HP-UX, and Windows NT. Sybase web.sql is directly linked with Web servers so it supports in-line scripting, embedding SQL commands, and Perl scripts in HTML documents. Most early solutions for Web/SQL connectivity relied on Perl and CGI helper programs. Those solutions tended to be ponderous, which may explain why most SQL vendors are working on Java and other solutions. Sybase plans to support Java with release 2.0 of web.sql.

A variety of vendors have developed Web-enabled query or report-generation products that use ODBC drivers. Seagate Crystal Services has updated Crystal Reports to publish reports via HTTP and HTML. Allaire's Cold Fusion uses HTML forms and supplemental Database Markup Language (DBML) tags, including suffixes to identify required fields. Aspect Software Engineering's dbWeb, Integral Results' iResults DataWeb, Intelligent Environments' Amazon, and Nomad's WebDBC provide gateways, HTML-forms extensions, or both.

WebObjects, Live Wire Pro, and SQLWindows

NeXT Software's WebObjects provides data access using an innovative, distributed-object approach. It supports multitier, distributed database applications by permitting a developer to partition logic and move elements such as business rules to application servers. WebObjects developers can configure any number of application servers to support an HTTP server. Web Objects servers work with ActiveX Automation clients, Java clients, and OLE distributed component objects (DCOM). WebObjects Enterprise includes objects that wrap legacy data from mainframe databases.

Netscape's SuiteSpot server package comprises site-management software and a developer's package, LiveWire Pro, that includes a Java-compatible scripting language and SQL database connectivity. Netscape supports enterprise and workgroup SQL databases from Informix, Oracle, Sybase, and Microsoft. LiveWire Pro also includes a single-user developer version of an SQL database and the ability to connect to ODBC databases. Database connectivity is only one part of the intranet requirement list, so Hewlett-Packard and Netscape recently partnered to produce intranet work group collaboration software for UNIX and Windows NT.

Centura Software (formerly Gupta) is adding Web-development features to SQLWindows. Centura Team Developer can generate two- and three-tier applications and Java applets. SQLWindows ships with a library of Quick Objects that includes new components for Web development. SQLWindows' Internet Quick Objects includes HTML display, FTP file transfer, HTTP protocol, and peer-to-peer communication objects. Centura Web Data Publisher lets developers create Web-based applications and forms that access SQL data without using HTML or CGI programming. Centura is also adding an Application Server to support three-tier applications.

Java Database Programming

Most operating-system vendors license Java, and Sun is developing a number of service APIs for Java developers. Java is appealing as a database developer's language because it is multithreaded, includes sockets for client-server programming and is highly portable. Java programs can be applets or applications, and Java compiles to bytecode so an application or applet executes in the presence of the Java Virtual Machine that interprets the bytecode. Developers can use sockets to easily write clients and servers with Java. Clients use a `Socket` object and the server uses a `ServerSocket` object. For each connection, the server creates a new thread and a new `Connection` object.

Many developers are looking to Java as a language for scalable applications. A number of two-tier, client/server tools have sufficient power for departmental and workgroup applications because they demand fewer resources than enterprise applications. Large intranets and Web applications are the most demanding because they must support many concurrent database connections. As two-tier client/server applications start running out of power, developers use some form of application partitioning such as database stored procedures and distributing logic to application servers. Java's multithreaded architecture positions it to be a useful tool for high-performance, distributed applications. Performance is a problem today, but a new generation of compilers is expected to close the gap between Java and languages such as C++.

The widespread deployment of SQL databases made integrating SQL into Java programs inevitable. To access SQL databases, some Java developers use native APIs but the industry is likely to coalesce around ODBC and JDBC. ODBC is ubiquitous, Java is ubiquitous, and JDBC appears to be on the same road. SQL programmers can find products that provide Java classes to wrap native APIs but product availability for multiple platforms is likely to be an issue. To write highly interoperable SQL programs, developers shun proprietary-database APIs and opt for classes such as JDBC or XDB Systems' JETConnect Pro.

JETConnect encapsulates ODBC, while Sun's JDBC is an SQL API that abstracts a subset of ODBC's capabilities. ODBC is a call-level interface, but JDBC includes Java classes that lay objects over the SQL programming process. The benefit of the JDBC and JETConnect classes is that they simplify SQL application development. For example, both include classes for working with timestamps, dates, and floating-point data types. Classes that encapsulate types include the type definition and the methods to operate on the type. JDBC and JETConnect are likely to use many of the same drivers. JDBC applications will be able to use bridge software to connect to ODBC drivers. There are approximately 80 companies with ODBC drivers, so the JDBC-ODBC Bridge will be a vital resource while the industry awaits JDBC drivers.

XDB Java Enterprise Tools

XDB Systems (Columbia, MD) is a DBMS vendor that saw Java's potential as a tool for enterprise developers. XDB's Java Enterprise Tools (JET) include JETConnect, Java classes that abstract the ODBC 2.0 API. XDB distributed a beta version with the intention of selling JETConnect as a separate product but then decided to offer the ODBC classes only as part of JETConnect Pro, which also supports JDBC and data-aware controls. JETConnect Pro clients communicate with JETConnect Pro on the server via a daemon or Windows NT service. XDB has implemented JETConnectPro so that it is usable with applets as well as applications. JETConnect Pro programs can operate with JDBC drivers as well as 32-bit ODBC drivers. XDB plans product releases to support JETConnect Pro on servers running Windows 95, Windows NT, Solaris, HP UX, AIX, Macintosh, and SGI operating systems. David Smith of XDB reports that the company is planning to provide support for "100% of ODBC 3.0 when it is available."

JETConnect maintains persistent connections to the SQL database. By caching connections, an application can eliminate the overhead of establishing connections for each request. JETConnect wraps ODBC so it provides features such as positioned UPDATEs and DELETEs, scrollable cursors, and row-wise and column-wise binding. ODBC uses handles to track resources that correspond to the application environment, database connections, and SQL statements. JETConnect uses a class to encapsulate methods and data related to the environment, connections, and statements. This is consistent with my C++ classes for ODBC (see "A Generic SQL Class Library," *Dr. Dobb's Sourcebook of Windows Programming*, Fall 1993).

JETConnect's `DbEnv` class corresponds to the environment, `DbDbC` corresponds to a connection, and `DbStmt` corresponds to a statement. JETConnect also includes a `DbException` class for error handling. When the `DbEnv`, `DbDbc`,

User Interface Classes	"Bound Data" Classes
`JetButton`	`JetColumnLink`
`JetImageField`	`JetDatabase`
`JetLabel`	`JetQuery`
`JetPanel`	`JetTableLink`
`JetTable Box`	`JetTransaction`
`JetTextField`	

Table 1: *XDB Systems' JETControls classes.*

or DbStmt methods throw an exception, DbException handles the return code, SQLError, and SQLSTATE processing. JETConnect also provides classes that encapsulate ODBC data types such as binary (DbBinary), date (DbDate), and integers (DbInteger). DbDataSource encapsulates ODBC data-source processing, while DbColDesc represents column descriptions. JETConnect uses the DbParamDesc class for parameter information and the DbDriver class to provide driver attributes and descriptive information. JETConnect encapsulates all ODBC 2.x functions in methods of DbEnv, DbDbc, DbStmt, or DbException.

The flow of a JETConnect application is similar to that of an ODBC application. To query a data source, instantiate the environment (DBEnv) and connection (DbDbC) objects to use the SQLConnect method. ODBC connection and statement options govern behavior so you can control your applet or application by calling the SQLSetConnectOption method for connections and SQLSetStmtOption method for statements. For example, some drivers provide the ability to use server-side cursors implemented by the SQL engine. Where native cursors are available, an application or applet can improve performance by using an option to bypass ODBC's client-side cursor library and use native cursors. After connecting to a data source, an application or applet typically instantiates a statement (DbStmt), binds columns to storage (SQLBindCol), and submits an SQL command. JETConnect supports several types of requests, including ad-hoc queries, prepared (compiled) queries, and stored procedures. JETConnect data-type classes can simplify a program when a statement executes and the program processes the result set. Applications and applets follow a similar process to retrieve metadata.

Windows visual programming fostered the growth of data-aware controls. Data-aware, or "bound" controls, associate database columns with memory variables and visual components. JETConnect Pro provides data-aware controls by extending Java's Abstract Window Toolkit. JETControls include a data-aware grid (TableBox), text boxes, and text fields. JETConnect Pro also supports Query and Update by Forms. Table 1 lists XDB's user-interface and data-aware controls classes.

Listing One is a simple Java application (testsoun.java) that demonstrates how to get feature information for a DBMS or ODBC driver. Using ODBC's SQLGetInfo function, one of several ODBC functions used to write adaptive programs, testsoun demonstrates how a Java application can determine whether the SQL for a specific data source includes the SOUNDEX scalar function. After instantiating information, environment, and connection objects, the program uses the TestForSOUNDEX method to determine whether SQLGetInfo reports that SOUNDEX is or is not supported. Note that testsoun is an application, not an applet. JETConnect applets include a URL parameter when invoking the SQLAllocEnv method.

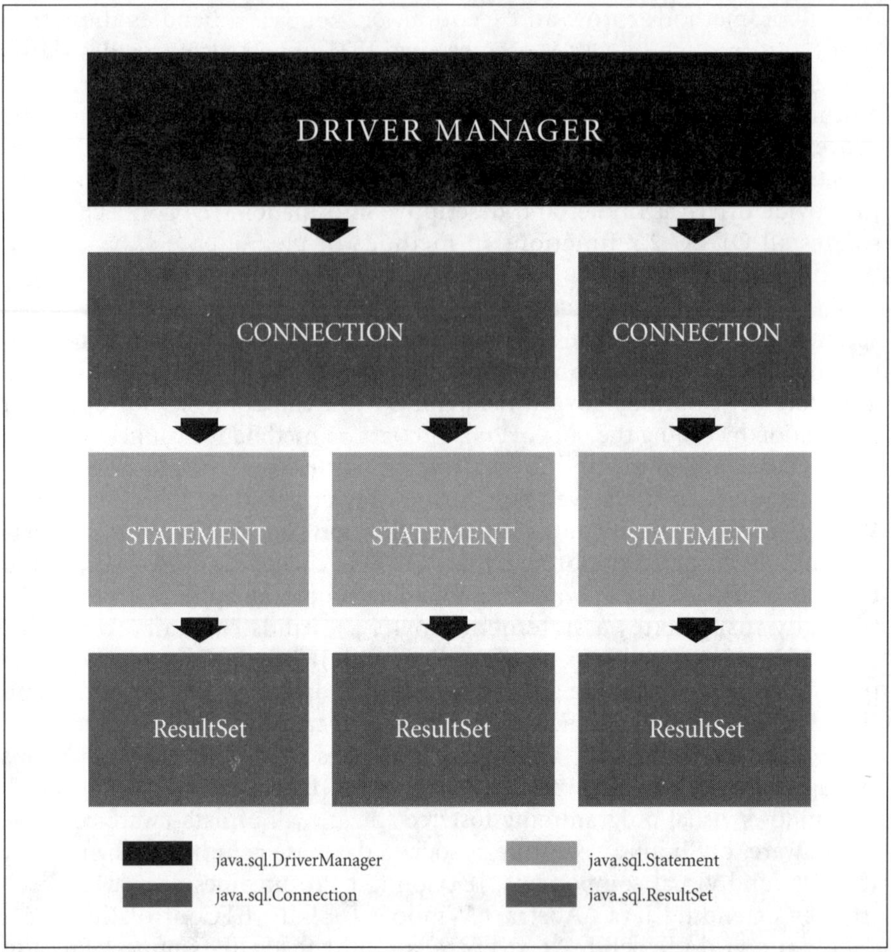

Figure 1: ***The relationship between JDBC's Driver Manager, Connection, and Statement objects.***

JDBC

Java Database Connectivity (JDBC) is an SQL API that includes Java classes, a driver manager, and loadable database drivers. The driver contains the logic required to access desktop databases or communicate with SQL servers and gateways. JDBC and ODBC are both based on the Call Level Interface (CLI) from X/Open that advanced to become the international standard CLI for SQL-92. Sun implemented JDBC by adding classes that provide an object layer over ODBC, much as Microsoft did with Data Access Objects. The list of companies developing for JDBC includes Oracle, Sybase, Informix, IBM, Centura (Gupta), Visigenic, Intersolv, OpenLink, OpenHorizon, Object Design, and SAS Institute.

The JDBC architecture includes a driver manager, although most JDBC calls go directly to loadable drivers. Java applications can use drivers for either specific databases or JDBC servers. JDBC and ODBC servers provide a thin client architecture that uses a single network transport and driver to connect to a server or gateway that provides links to multiple SQL servers. For added flexibility, the JDBC Driver Manager can also use the JDBC-ODBC Bridge to connect to ODBC drivers. The bridge, jointly developed by JavaSoft and Intersolv, maps JDBC logic into the appropriate ODBC function calls. It includes a series of portable object classes written in Java and installs as a dynamic link library (DLL) for Windows NT, Windows 95, and Solaris 2.4 and above. Many JDBC calls will go directly to JDBC drivers, but when a program uses the JDBC-ODBC Bridge, all ODBC function calls go to the ODBC Driver Manager.

The JDBC class hierarchy begins with a Driver Manager class derived from Java's base object class. The java.sql.DriverManager interface supports driver loading, and opening connections (`getConnection`) and is the counterpart to the ODBC environment. The Driver Manager is an application-level object, so there is only one instance per application. Applications may use multiple connections, so the connection class (`java.sql.Connection`) is derived from the Driver Manager class. Some DBMS products support multiple SQL statements per connection; therefore, JDBC allows multiple statements (`java.sql.Statement`) to be derived from a connection. Figure 1 shows the relationship of these classes.

JDBC supports stored procedures and the prepare-and-execute model for SQL statement execution. Preparing is somewhat analogous to compiling an SQL statement and is more efficient for repetitive queries. JDBC programs will use the `java.sql.PreparedStatement` interface for prepared queries and `java.sql.CallableStatement` for procedures. The `java.sql.ResultSet` object represents a result set, the rows returned for an SQL query. Programmers use `java.sql.ResultSet` to do row-level processing of results. The `ResultSet` maintains a cursor and provides `get` methods (for example, `getString`, `getInteger`) to permit an application to traverse a result set a row at a time. Instead of ODBC-style binding and fetching, an application will execute a query and then use `ResultSet getXXX` methods to get the values for columns. JDBC provides the capability for an application to access result-set columns by name or index.

JDBC includes classes such as `java.sql.Numeric`, `java.sql.Date`, and `java.sql.Time` to support SQL data types. It also supports large binary and character objects by using i/o streams (`java.io.InputStream`). JDBC supports Unicode and ASCII characters and provides runtime information about types and features. The `java.sql.DatabaseMetaData` class is analogous to ODBC's `SQLGetInfo` function because both provide information about database capabilities (such as, whether a DBMS supports outer joins).

JDBC and ODBC support entry-level SQL-92 and extend SQL by using the same escape clauses, so SQL statements should be interoperable between JDBC and ODBC drivers. JDBC provides a basic implementation of unscrollable cursors. Programs can obtain the cursor associated with a result set and then use the cursor name in positioned `UPDATE` and `DELETE` operations. JDBC doesn't support ODBC bookmarks, which permit an application to mark its place in a result set and return to that location later.

A trace of the SQL sent from application to driver can be a valuable debugging resource. It is no surprise that JDBC provides a logging facility for the Driver Manager and drivers. JavaSoft will provide a suite of JDBC compliance tests to certify driver and application compliance.

Metadata and Adaptive Programming

To write code that is interoperable or portable across a variety of DBMS back ends, an application developer must use adaptive programming techniques. A program should determine at execution time what available features affect the logic of a program. This includes information such as supported SQL and data types, whether the SQL supports outer joins, whether the DBMS preserves the cursor context on a COMMIT or ROLLBACK, whether nulls sort low or high, and so on. Adaptive techniques involve coding to make runtime decisions, but the payoff is highly interoperable code that doesn't have to be recompiled or relinked when the program must operate against a new database or when a DBMS adds new data types. ODBC provides functions (such as `SQLGetInfo` and `SQLGetTypeInfo`) to return information about data types, database, and DBMS features. JDBC's metadata interfaces provide methods that return information used for execution-time decisions. The metadata interfaces are `java.sql.DatabaseMetaData` and `java.sql.Resultset-MetaData`. Some metadata methods, such as `supportsExtendedSQLGrammar`, return a Boolean (`true` or `false`); others, such as `getMaxColumnsInIndex`, return an integer. Still others return a string (`getSQLKeywords`). Because metadata processing is often comparable to processing data, JDBC defines some metadata methods that return a `ResultSet` type. ODBC programs often use a loop to process data or metadata result sets, but JDBC wraps that logic in methods such as `getPrimaryKeys` that return the result set. For some metadata, JDBC provides a simpler solution than ODBC. For example, JDBC will enumerate the list of available scalar functions of each type, whereas ODBC requires calls to `SQLGetInfo` to check whether individual functions are available.

SQL Tools for Java

JDBC and JETConnect are not the only game in town for Java database programmers. Products such as Spider's NetDynamics, Jagg Systems' ODBC Engine, and Open Horizon Connection support Java SQL applications. Jagg Systems' ODBC Engine provides a `Jagg` class that extends java.object. `Jagg` uses a single method (execSQL) for each SQL statement. It returns results by entering results in a Vector, one Vector element per row of the result set. Queries return each row as a String with fields separated by a configurable separator. The return value indicates success or failure. Open Horizon Connection provides links to ODBC or JDBC clients and supports the Open System Foundations' Distributed Computing Environment (DCE). Connection also includes an object broker (Connection Application Broker) that supports three-tier development by moving business rules to application servers. Transarc Corp. recently supplemented its transaction processing and DCE products by adding a Java-development toolkit. DE-Light Web Client lets Java clients use DCE Remote Procedure Calls and interface to the Transarc Encina TP monitor.

Borland has announced a new InterBase client that will be available before the end of 1996. The InterBase Client is a Java application, and it supports JDBC, so it should be a multiplatform client. IBM and Oracle are involved in major Java data-access activities. IBM's Data Java is in development, while Oracle will support Java integration with Developer 2000 and Project Sedona, a repository of OLE, Open Doc, and Java components. WebLogic's dbKona provides database connectivity for Java applications (nonapplets). It provides an object interface to Oracle, Sybase, and SQL Server 6.0, and supports multiple, heterogeneous connections. It uses native APIs and vendor-supplied network libraries. WebLogic is also working on dbKona/T3, a product for developing three-tier applications.

Distributed or Remote Objects

No discussion of data access today can omit the trend toward partitioned or distributed applications. JavaSoft is working on APIs that provide Java applications the ability to use remote procedures (remote methods) and object brokers. JavaSoft is working on the JavaIDL system for distributed programming by connecting to Object Request Brokers, while Java RMI is the API for Remote Method Invocation. Remote Method Invocation lets you define a remote interface that inherits from `sunw.rmi.RemoteObject`. After you compile the method definition with a stub generator called rmigen, your Java client can invoke methods on remote servers. JavaIDL lets you use Object Management Group's Interface Definition Language (IDL) to define shared objects. To create objects, you compile definitions with idlgen to generate client and server stubs and Java interface definitions. A Java client can then invoke an IDL object at a remote server.

End Notes

Microsoft has taken a number of steps to integrate the Internet with its Windows solutions. It has licensed Java to integrate into its operating system and into Internet Explorer, its unified browser and operating-system shell. Microsoft's Java compiler will share capabilities with other Microsoft languages, including an HTML forms engine, the ability to produce and use ActiveX controls, and the ability to create and use active documents. Space does not permit an examination of ActiveX, but Microsoft is extending Object

Linking and Embedding to ease object access on the Internet and intranets. Microsoft includes an ODBC-compatible database connector with its Internet Information Server and will soon release ActiveX objects that provide access to relational and nonrelational databases.

Developers that must support databases on the Web—or networks based on Web technology—have many options. Distributed-object technologies and database APIs are likely to play an important role in developing distributed applications.

Listing One

```
/
 FILE NAME:  testsoun.java     TITLE: test for SOUNDEX scalar function

 AUTHOR:  K. E. North II, Resource Group, Inc.

 Copyright (c) Kendall E. North II, 1996. All rights reserved. Reproduction
 or translation of this work beyond that permitted in Section 117 of the
 United States Copyright Act without express written permission of the
 copyright owner is unlawful.
 The purchaser may make backup copies for his/her own use only and not for
 distribution or resale. The Author and Publisher assume no responsibility
 errors, omissions or damages caused by the use of these programs or from
 use of the information contained herein.

 SYNOPSIS:

/

import jet.connect.;


class TestSoundex
{
    static GetConnectInfo info;
    static DbValue              IsSupported = new DbValue();
    static DbEnv                environment       = null;
    static DbDbc                connection   = null;
    static DbStmt               statement  = null;


    public static void main(String args[])
    {
       info = new GetConnectInfo(args);
       try
       {
           environment  = DbEnv.SQLAllocEnv();
           connection  = environment.SQLAllocConnect();
           connection.SQLConnect(info.Server(),info.UserId(),info.Password());
           TestForSOUNDEX();
       }
```

```
        catch (Exception e)
        {
            System.out.println(e.toString());
        }
        finally
        {

            if (connection != null)
            {
                connection.SQLDisconnect();
                connection.SQLFreeConnect();
            }

            if (environment != null)
                environment.SQLFreeEnv();
        }
    }


    static void TestForSOUNDEX()
    {
        connection.SQLGetInfo(Db.SQL_STRING_FUNCTIONS, IsSupported);

        if ((IsSupported.intValue() & Db.SQL_FN_STR_SOUNDEX) ==
                                    Db.SQL_FN_STR_SOUNDEX)
            System.out.println("Data source implements SOUNDEX");
        else
            System.out.println("Data source does not provide SOUNDEX");
    }
}
```

Database Programming with JDBC

Erin Carroll and Andrew Wilson

The Java language, touted for being highly portable, was lacking a major component until recently. Database connectivity in today's Information Age must certainly be considered a major component of any programming model. To meet this requirement, JavaSoft has recently introduced the JDBC API (Application Programming Interface) for database access as flexible and portable as Java code.

The JDBC API was developed to have a standard, ODBC-like (Open Database Connectivity) interface that will allow Java-application developers access to databases residing on different servers—with different database management systems—in much the same way as ODBC. The plan was to use drivers that interpret standard JDBC syntax into native Database Management System (DBMS) syntax. From a development point of view, the underlying platform and DBMS are not very relevant, as Java is portable and uses drivers

---

Erin and Andy are engineers at NuMega Technologies, Inc. They can be reached at erinc@numega.com and andyw@numega.com, respectively. *Reprinted courtesy of* Web Techniques.

that deal with the underlying DBMS. This removes concerns about DBMS specifics from the application developer's task list.

The drivers that translate from JDBC to native DBMS must be ANSI SQL-2 entry-level compliant. JDBC also supports pass-through, where the Structured Query Language (SQL) syntax is passed directly to the database engine without translation at the driver level. As far as JDBC is concerned, this basically means anything goes; the underlying DBMS will handle the syntax.

This is important, because even with a standard API, each DBMS may provide extensions that will allow for optimization of the particular engine. For example, Database B provides the minimal functionality to be ODBC compliant, but Database A has functionality not covered or required in the ODBC specifications. In this case, the pass-through option may be chosen to use the special features of Database A, even though it limits the portability of the code being developed.

The JDBC API Opens Up Your Java Applications

The JDBC API is a low-level, generic SQL API that will provide the flexibility needed for developing Java applications connecting to different DBMS engines, enterprise-wide or across the Internet. This interface provides application developers with a SQL-compliant interface much like the Microsoft API, so no additional learning curve is necessary for database development in Java.

According to JavaSoft, the JDBC API was modeled after the Microsoft ODBC API. Both are based on the Microsoft, X\Open SQL Call Level Interface (CLI). Open database connectivity means that applications are not limited to "talking" to one driver that is connected to one database. Rather, an application may be connected to multiple databases residing on multiple servers using different DBMS engines. This means you can create an applet to connect to your favorite-vacation-spots database, while querying your busy calendar-of-important-events database. Point, click and violà! You can schedule a week in Tahiti right after you finish your next big project.

OK, maybe this small example doesn't adequately illustrate the endless possibilities. Just imagine you are an information provider with huge databases distributed across many different platforms. Your task is to provide your customers with simple, usable, limited access to the data they require. Your job just got easier.

Although ODBC is a good solution for connectivity in other languages, the addition of the JDBC is necessary for database connectivity through Java because the ODBC is a C interface, making it inappropriate for Java access. JavaSoft states that:

> **calls from Java to native C code have a number of drawbacks in the security, implementation, robustness, and automatic portability of applications.**

The Big Beans of the JDBC

The JDBC API has been implemented as a group of interfaces that allow connection, execution of SQL statements, and result-set processing by communicating with a database via the JDBC Driver Manager and DBMS-specific driver. JavaSoft lists the following as the most important JDBC API interfaces:

- `java.sql.DriverManager`: loads drivers and supports new database connections.
- `java.sql.Connection`: represents a connection to a database.
- `java.sql.Statement`: holds a SQL statement to be executed.
- `java.sql.ResultSet`: provides access to the result set of a `java.sql.Statement`.

Open Database Connectivity

Much like the ODBC architecture, the JDBC is comprised of a single, common interface, DBMS-specific drivers, and a Driver Manager. Placed between the Java application and the JDBC drivers, one of the Driver Manager's jobs is to establish the connection between the appropriate driver and the Java application. When the Driver Manager receives a request to connect to a specific URL, it will attempt to locate a driver able to connect to the database at that URL. A driver list is consulted when there are multiple drivers that may connect to a given database. The list of drivers is configured by the user and a driver is selected by the JDBC Driver Manager based on the order and security of the driver in the list.

Developers may elect to eliminate the Driver Manager from the driver-selection process, because applications are allowed to connect directly to a particular driver without going through the database-management layer. However, in either scenario, it is the responsibility of the driver, once it has been loaded, to register with the JDBC Driver Manager.

Currently, the only driver available is the beta version of Intersolv's JDBC-ODBC Bridge Driver, built "on top of ODBC." The Bridge Driver has been implemented as a DLL that maps JDBC functions to ODBC calls. According to Intersolv, this design will allow any ODBC driver—compliant with version 2.0 and above—to be used with the JDBC-ODBC Bridge Driver.

True open connectivity will be realized when vendors eventually create JDBC drivers that contain implementations of the abstract classes that are provided by the JDBC API and will allow connections through the Driver Manager to many different DBMS engines.

The initial implementation of the JDBC does not include support for the following:

- Committing transactions across different connections.
- Scrollable cursors.
- ODBC-style bookmarks.

Writing an JDBC-Enabled Applet

The demonstration applet is pretty straightforward. It attaches to a data source and allows us to do a series of queries, updates, inserts, and deletes. It's very short and fairly simple to read.

Though the applet is simple, setting up the JDBC so that an applet can be written is by far the hardest part. There are several small items to keep in mind. If the system is not set up correctly, many odd problems that make little or no sense may result. Almost all of these report back a message stating something similar to "No suitable driver found."

The first consideration is our CLASSPATH. JDK 1.0.2 requires that `CLASSPATH` point to \JAVA\LIB\CLASSES.ZIP, but we need to expand that so it also points to the directory of our JDBC install and the location of our JDBC-ODBC bridge. Ours, for example, is "set CLASSPATH=C:\JAVA\LIB \CLASSES.ZIP;C:\JAVA\JDBC\CLASSES;C:\JAVA\JDBC-ODBC\CLASSES." This allows us to just compile our applet and load various classes needed at run time.

In order for the JDBC-ODBC bridge to work, we need to load a JDBCODBC.DLL. This DLL is located under the JDBC-ODBC\CLASSES\JDBC\ODBC directory. Either copy the DLL into a directory your PATH environment currently points to or add the new path to your current PATH settings. The latter is a better choice, since the JDBC-ODBC bridge might be updated several more times and this will help avoid mismatched DLLs and classes. Your applet will not work until you do this.

Finally, we need to create a data source. Windows NT and 95 have an ODBC-setup option in the control panels, which can create a new system data source. You must do this so that the JDBC can actually communicate to the database using the bridge. The reason will become apparent later on.

Listing One shows our applet's class-member variable declarations and our `include` statements. There are three new types we have not seen before: `Connection`, `Statement`, and `ResultSet`. `Connection` is pretty obvious: It establishes a connection to a data source. `Statement` is used to pass an SQL statement to the ODBC driver. `ResultSet` stores the returned information from the ODBC driver. These new types are added when we import java.sql.*.

After initializing the user interface, we need to connect to the database. But first, we need to load the JDBC-ODBC driver and test it; see Listing Two. We load the driver using the `Class.forName` method, which loads the class and keeps it resident in memory until the applet terminates. We then test the driver with the method `Driver.jdbcCompliant`, which will return `TRUE` if the driver does follow the JDBC specification. Finally, we check the driver to confirm that it can attach to the data source's URL. Once we know that it will work, we can actually attach to the database.

The URL for a data source is broken down into three parts, each separated by colons and the entire string in quotes. The first part, JDBC, represents the interface. The subprotocol name is the second part; in our case this will be

ODBC. The final part is the subname, which is the data source's name. In our example, this entire URL will read jdbc:odbc:TestDB.

Once we have a valid URL, we can attempt to connect to the database using the `DriverManager.getConnection` method. This function will attempt to attach to the URL using each driver loaded. In our case it will use the JdbcOdbcDriver and return a new `Connection` class. With that connection we can then generate a new `Statement` class, which will allow us to actually query the database; see Listing Three.

The `Statement` class does all the work, sending the SQL string to the actual data source's driver through the JDBC-ODBC bridge. We do this by calling `Statement.executeQuery`, which returns a `ResultSet`. There is also another method, `Statement.executeUpdate`, which we use to insert, delete, or update a row within our datasource. It's important to understand that the `Statement` class is what allows us to make queries of the database. Everything prior to this simply establishes a communication session.

The `ResultSet` class is used to interpret the row(s) we just received. We may have several rows in a single `ResultSet`, so before we can process anything, we need to move to the right row by calling `ResultSet.next`. Initially we are on a blank row, and any manipulation of this blank row will raise a `SQLException`. Each time we query the data source, we must move to the next row before we try to read the data. Moving beyond the last row also raises a `SQLException`. Assuming we don't raise an exception, we should be able to read the data from the row and display it in our applet, shown in Listing Four.

The ability to read is significant; however, we need to add some functionality so that we can do more than just look at our database. `Statement.executeUpdate` inserts, deletes, and updates rows in our database. We need specify only the correct SQL string to pass to the ODBC driver to carry out our task. Listing Five shows how we delete a record from the database.

Another useful function is the ability to scroll through the database. Listing Six shows the Next and Previous buttons in action. Next works fairly simply; Previous, however, is a little trickier since it involves going backward through the row list. A minor inconvenience of the JDBC is that the database is not scrollable, which means that you can only move forward in the database. To move backward, you need to issue a new SQL statement and trap the `ResultSet`.

Finally, we should clean up our connections during the termination of the applet. `Connection`, `Statement`, and `ResultSet` all have close functions that explicitly close each layer's interaction with the database; see Listing Seven. This makes your code more readable to other users. Further, by explicitly closing your JDBC services, you guarantee that another Java interpreter will not inadvertently leave your database open after the applet has terminated.

This sample application, although basic, provides the framework needed to access databases using Java and the JDBC API. Using this as a starting point, you can now go on and create your own platform-independent database applications.

Java Continues to Mature

Java can be looked at in two different ways. The first is as a programming language, with characteristics such as organization, syntax, mechanics, and construction. The second is as its application, with the ability to apply the language in a variety of different applications and products. Java as a language is very powerful and fairly easy for the average C++ developer to learn, cutting the learning curve dramatically, while it has tremendous support for graphics, GUI interfaces, multiple threads, sound, file I/O, and exception handling.

If all this functionality sounds familiar, it's because the Microsoft Foundation Classes (MFC) had much of it back in the days of Visual C++ 1.0. With time, Microsoft expanded the MFC to include things that made it easier to write more complex code, such as OLE, WINSOCK, and ODBC connectivity. Now MFC can significantly reduce the time it takes to write an application because so many of the critical classes are included.

Java had many classes included from the beginning, such as networking and a multitude of good exception classes. However, it needed to take another step to make it a viable developer solution. New classes have been added, one of the most important being the JDBC, giving us connectivity to the databases that drive our various businesses and reducing the time it would have taken to code the interface ourselves.

The JDBC has a significant impact upon daily business. The JDBC can give us access to any one of our databases, bringing it online with minimal effort. We can add more robust user-friendly interfaces, and we can trust the exception handling in Java not to crash our server when a fault occurs. Finally, we can reduce the time that it takes to implement a Web and/or database solution.

The JDBC is another step in making Java one of the most powerful languages available. It currently gives us more connectivity than anyone would ever want to code themselves. It provides a common code that can be run on any platform, eliminating the old concept of porting from Windows to UNIX, which never seemed to look or work remotely like the original-platform version. It now gives us access to a variety of databases and expands the range of supported applications.

As developers, we need to make a decision about Java. Do we continue to look at Java as a language that we keep locked away in the Internet, or do we start to put together full applications using Java, knowing that it has many, if not all, of the features of MFC? Many of us use MFC in the applications we write or run. Knowing that we can write the same applications in Java—and that it will work in the same way on all platforms—how long will it be before we switch? Will we switch before our competitors?

Listing One

```
import java.applet.*;
import java.awt.*;
import java.net.URL;
import java.util.*;
import java.sql.*;

public class JDBCSAMP extends Applet
{

       String DBurl = "jdbc:odbc:TestDB";
       String query = "SELECT * FROM Animals";


       Connection connection;
       Statement statement;
       ResultSet results;
```

Listing Two

```
Class Tmp;
try{Tmp = Class.forName ("jdbc.odbc.JdbcOdbcDriver");}
       catch(ClassNotFoundException ex)
       {
              txtDesc.setText("ClassNotFoundException: "+ex.getMessage());
              return false;
       }

Driver d;
try{d = (Driver) Tmp.newInstance();}
       catch(Exception ex)
{
       txtDesc.setText("Exception: "+ex.getMessage());
       return false;
       }

if(d.jdbcCompliant() == false)
       {
       txtDesc.setText("Driver not JDBC compliant!");
       return false;
       }

try{
if(d.acceptsURL(DBurl)== false)
              {
              txtDesc.setText("Won't accept!");
              return false;
              }
```

Listing Three

```
Connection connection = DriverManager.getConnection (DBurl);
statement = connection.createStatement();
results = statement.executeQuery(query);
```

Listing Four

```
public void DispNextRow()
{
try
{
results.next();
       nID = results.getInt(1);
       txtName.setText(results.getString(2));
       txtHabitat.setText(results.getString(3));
       txtDesc.setText(results.getString(4));
}
catch (SQLException ex)
       {
       return;
       }

}
```

Listing Five

```
public void DeleteAnimal()
{

String Update;

try
{
       Update = "DELETE FROM ANIMALS where ID="+nID;

       int row = statement.executeUpdate(Update);
       if( row == 0)
              {
              lblHeading.setText("Delete Failed");
              return;
              }
       lblHeading.setText("Row: "+row);

       results = statement.executeQuery(query);
       DispNextRow();

       }
```

```
catch (SQLException ex)
       {
       return;
       }
}
```

Listing Six

```
if("Next".equals(arg))
       {
       try
{
              nPrevID = nID;
results = statement.executeQuery("SELECT * FROM ANIMALS
WHERE ID >"+nPrevID);
              } catch (SQLException ex) {return true;}
       DispNextRow();
       }
else if("Previous".equals(arg))
       {
       nID—;
       try
       {
              results = statement.executeQuery("SELECT * FROM ANIMALS
WHERE ID="+nID);
              DispNextRow();
              }
       catch (SQLException ex)
              {
              return true;
              }
       }
```

Listing Seven

```
public void stop()
{
System.out.println("I'm done!");
try
       {
              results.close();
              statement.close();
              connection.close();
       }
catch (SQLException ex)
       {
              txtDesc.setText("SQLException: "+ex.getMessage());
       }
}
```

The Oracle Call Interface and C++

Jeremy Woo-Sam and Tony Murphy

The Oracle Call Interface (OCI) allows C applications to access and manipulate data in an Oracle database. Unfortunately, using the C API functions requires extensive knowledge of your tables and their data types. You must also know how to access columns inside a table and efficiently retrieve database rows into an application. By creating abstractions for database access and manipulation, you can wrap the C API into C++ classes. This provides database access in an easy-to-use and easy-to-maintain form, promotes code reuse, and bridges RDBMS concepts to an object-oriented paradigm.

In this article, we will present DBObject, a C++ class library that provides database connectivity and query access to an Oracle RDBMS. In doing so, we will examine the interface classes that are used within a C++ application, and the implementation classes that support array fetching within the interface classes. We will use an example that supports some primary data types:

*Jeremy is the project leader of SQL*C++, and Tony is the project leader for SQR at MITI. They can be reached at jeremyw@miti.com and tonym@miti.com, respectively. Reprinted courtesy of* Dr. Dobb's Journal.

variable character strings, fixed-length character strings, numerics, and date types. Our abstraction of a database connection allows both local and remote connectivity, while our abstraction of database columns provides the mechanism for accessing data in the query.

The object-oriented approach offers database developers several benefits. For instance, users not familiar with cursors, array fetching, and other OCI concepts often find retrieving data from Oracle a time-consuming task. Object orientation lets users focus on solving their domain problems rather than on retrieving data.

Oracle data types are substantially different from those supported in C. This causes problems when converting between the database and C data types. For example, the Oracle NUMBER data type can have a value of NULL or 0. In the Oracle world, these values are different. This means no primitive C data type can entirely represent an Oracle NUMBER, because *float*, *double*, and *int* cannot represent both NULL and 0. This problem is commonly referred to as the "impedance mismatch" between RDBMS and C data types.

The common solution is to map the Oracle NUMBER data type to a C *struct*. However, this creates a new problem because you cannot use the C arithmetic operators with user-defined *structs*. (Note that C++ classes do allow *structs* to have operators.)

Finally, using high-level database abstractions lets you extend a class library's functionality without impacting existing applications. For example, the first version of our class did not implement array fetching; this was added

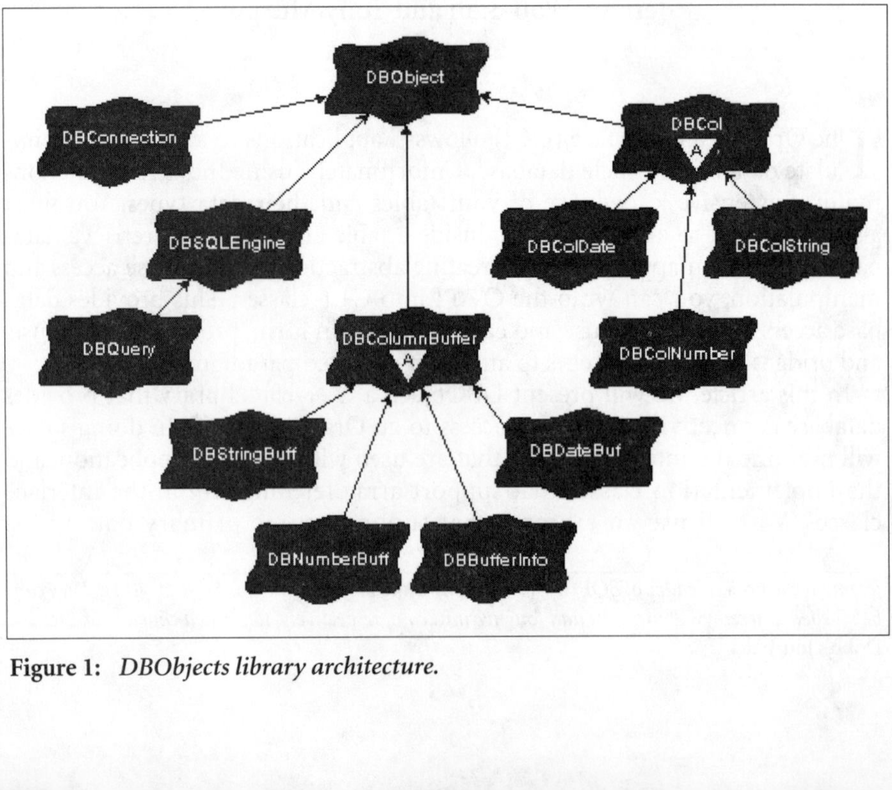

Figure 1: ***DBObjects library architecture.***

later to improve efficiency. Likewise, obsolete OCI calls can be replaced with their newer counterparts without changing any application code. And, since our abstractions are valid on most SQL databases, our class library can easily be ported to other relational databases.

The DBObject Classes

The DBObjects database class library has two layers: the interface layer and the implementation layer. Interface-layer classes are routinely used to retrieve information from Oracle; implementation-layer classes are used internally by the interface layer. Figure 1 shows the class hierarchy for DBObjects, while Figure 2 shows the implementation and interface layers.

The *DBObject* class is the base class. It handles local and database errors. The *DBConnection* class is an abstraction of a database connection; see Listing One. *DBConnection* encapsulates the OCI functions that let you log into an Oracle RDBMS; see Table 1. Multiple *DBConnection* objects can be created to

Function	Description
orlon	Establishes concurrent communication between an OCI program and an Oracle database.
ologof	Disconnects a login data area from the Oracle program global area and frees all Oracle resources owned by the Oracle user process.
ocom	Commits the current transaction.
ocon	Enables autocommit.
ocof	Disables autocommit.
orol	Rolls back current transaction.
oopen	Opens specified cursor.
oparse	Parses an SQL statement or PL/SQL block and associates it with a cursor.
ocan	Cancels a query after the desired number of rows have been fetched.
oclose	Disconnects a cursor from the data area in the Oracle server with which it is associated.
ofen	Fetches on multiple rows into arrays of variables, taking advantage of the Oracle array interface.
oexec	Executes the SQL statement associated with a cursor.
odescr	Describes select-list items for SQL queries.
odefin	Defines an output variable for a specified select-list item of an SQL query.
oerhms	Returns the text of an Oracle error message, given the error code.

Table 1: *OCI functions.*

access different local or remote data sources within a single application. Each time a *DBConnection* object is instantiated, it in turn creates and maintains an Oracle Login Cursor. The Oracle Login Cursor is deleted when the *DBConnection* object is destroyed.

Class *DBSQLEngine* encapsulates the database cursor and the OCI functions for parsing SQL statements. The class also describes column information in SELECT statements, defines the output buffers, and fetches rows from the database. The *DBQuery* class, which inherits from *DBSQLEngine*, takes a valid SELECT statement and retrieves rows for the SELECT statement. The member function *MoveNext()* provides the means of navigating through the rows of the query.

The abstract *DBCol* class provides the interface to the data in the *DBQuery* object. The derived type-specific classes format the data within *DBQuery* so that it can be manipulated or printed.

The *DBColumnBuffer* classes are implementation classes that support array fetching, which allows multiple rows to be fetched with a single database access. This technique greatly reduces network traffic and improves access to database rows. The *DBColumnBuffer* classes also contain information about the column, such as its position, name, width, data type, scale, and precision.

The Interface Layer

The interface layer is comprised of *DBConnection*, *DBQuery*, *DBCol*, *DBColNumber*, *DBColDate*, and *DBColString*. Each class is a well-defined abstraction of some aspect of the Oracle interface.

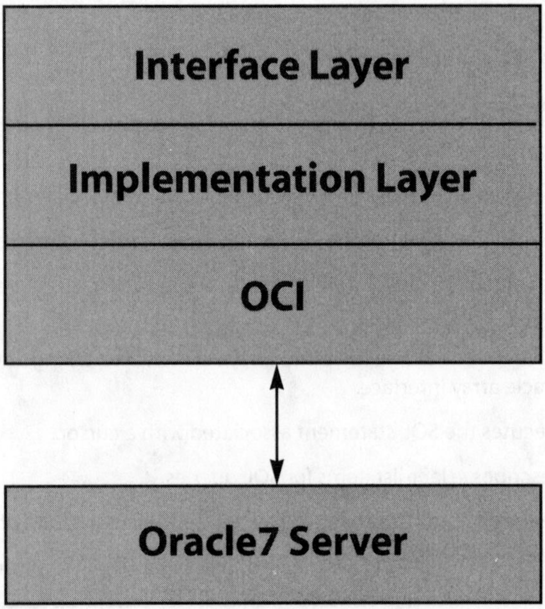

Figure 2: *The DBObjects class library.*

DBConnection manages the database connection. You simply instantiate an instance of the class by passing an Oracle connect string to the constructor to establish a connection with the database. When the object is destroyed (either explicitly or when it goes out of scope), the destructor severs the connection with the database. Behind the scenes, the OCI functions ORLON and OLOGOF are used to log on to and off of the Oracle server.

DBQuery abstracts the concept of an SQL query. Its constructor accepts an SQL string as a parameter. To execute the query, invoke the *Execute()* member function. The rows of data returned by the query can be sequenced using the *MoveNext()* member function.

Internally, the *DBQuery* object uses an instance of *DBSQLEngine* to parse the SQL statement. It allocates *DBColumnBuffers* to hold the columns retrieved from the database by the SQL string. *DBQuery* uses the OCI function ODESCR to decide which type of column buffer to use: *DBNumberBuff*, *DBDateBuff*, or *DBBufferInfo*.

DBCol classes are used to interface and manipulate the actual data returned from the database. *DBColNumber*, *DBColDate*, and *DBColString* implement the C++ equivalents to the Oracle NUMBER, DATE, and CHAR data types, respectively.

DBCol is an abstract base class for the column classes that implements services required by *DBColNumber*, *DBColDate*, and *DBColString*. Such services include maintaining a pointer to the *DBQuery* object, identifying the corresponding *DBColumnBuffer* that contains the physical data, and implementing an *IsNull()* member function to tell if a column's value is set to NULL.

Interoperability of Column Objects

Implementing a cast to *double* in *DBColNumber* lets you use instances of this type with C arithmetic operators. For example, *Total=A+B* is legal in C++, where *A* and *B* are of type *DBColNumber* or *double*, and *Total* is of type *double.* During arithmetic operations, a NULL column is assumed to be of value 0. However, if you prefer a value other than 0, simply inherit from *DBColNumber* and redefine the cast.

DBColString implements a cast to *char**, which allows its instances to interoperate with functions that require null-terminated strings. For example, *strcmp(A,B)* is acceptable in C++ if *A* and *B* are either of type *DBColString* or are pointers to null-terminated strings. During string function calls, a NULL value is converted to a null-terminated string of length 0. Users can implement their own representation of NULL by overloading the *DBColString::GetString()* member function.

The Implementation Layer

Implementation classes include *DBSQLEngine*, *DBColumnBuffer*, *DBStringBuffer*, *DBNumberBuffer*, and *DBDateBuffer*. They represent the internal structure and implementation of handling the rows retrieved from the database.

The *DBSQLEngine* class encapsulates the OCI functions that handle database cursors. These OCI functions handle fetching rows from the database, parsing the SQL statement, describing columns from a SELECT statement, and defining the memory area to hold rows returned from a database fetch. *DBSQLEngine* can be easily extended to support DML and DDL statements.

DBColumnBuffer is an abstract base class for *DBStringBuffer*, *DBNumberBuffer*, and *DBDateBuffer*. It represents the static and dynamic information of a database column and is responsible for gathering and maintaining information about it, including column type, external type, width, position, name, scale, and precision. *DBColumnBuffer* also contains information about the return length and NULL status for each row of the column. The pure virtual member functions *GetData()* and *GetBufferAddress()* are defined in the derived classes. This allows the derived classes to manage, maintain, and index their rows.

The Big Picture

The *DBConnection*, *DBQuery*, and *DBCol* classes work together to access data from the database. Separating these classes into complete, distinct abstractions allows greater flexibility than folding connectivity, query capabilities, and column handling into one class. Once a successful connection to the database is established, the *DBConnection* object can be used by multiple *DBQuery* objects. The *DBQuery* constructor takes the SELECT string and a reference to a *DBConnection* object as its arguments. When a *DBQuery* object has been successfully created, *DBCol* objects can be associated to the *DBQuery* internal columns. The *DBCol* objects take a reference to a *DBQuery* object and the column number that it wants to reference. Once "attached" to the *DBQuery* internal column, you can print and manipulate the *DBCol* object.

The *DBQuery* object constructs and maintains the *DBColumnBuffer* objects. It parses the SELECT statement and creates a linked list of *DBBufferInfo* objects for each column in the SELECT statement by calling the *DBSQLEngine::Describe()* function. A linked list is preferable to an array of *DBColumnBuffer* objects because Oracle does not provide any functions to determine the number of columns in a SELECT statement. To determine the number of columns in the query, the ODESCR function is called until it returns the end-of-select error status. While calling *DBSQLEngine::Describe()*, we gather information about the column to populate the *DBQuery* object's *DBColumnBuffer* array.

The *DBQuery* object now allocates an array of *DBColumnBuffer* pointers that reference a data-type-specific *DBColumnBuffer* object such as a *DBStringBuffer* or a *DBDateBuffer*. The *DBQuery* object walks the linked list, allocates a data-type-specific *DBColumnBuffer* object, copies the information from the linked list, and sets the proper width and external type.

After the array has been populated, the *DBQuery* object passes each *DBColumnBuffer* object in the array to the *DBSQLEngine* member function

Define(). This is done to determine the destination address for the rows retrieved.

Example 1 is a typical C++ application that establishes a connection and performs a SELECT on a table called "EMP" (see Example 2). When Example 1 is executed, the output shown in Example 3 is generated. The source code for *DBConnection*, *DBQuery*, and other classes is available electronically on the diskette.

Possible Extensions

To extend the DBObject class library, you could, for example, add enhanced data types. The DBObjects database class library demonstrates how to abstract a limited number of Oracle data types in C++. The same techniques can be applied to simulate other Oracle data types such as LONG and LONG RAW.

The current implementation utilizes double-precision floating-point numbers to represent the numeric values of NUMBER columns. This is sufficient for applications that don't require more than 15 digits of precision. Oracle itself supports a maximum precision of 38 digits. For more than 15 digits of precision, a high-precision column class could be developed. Client-application writers could then manage the efficiency-versus-precision trade-offs using the column class that most closely corresponds with their needs.

Additional member functions could be added to *DBColString*, *DBColNumber*, and *DBColDate*, resulting in more complete data types.

```
#include <iostream.h>
#include <dbobject.h>
#include <dbcol.h>
int main()
{
    DBConnection TestConn("scott/tiger@t:cire-ss2:oracle7");
    DBQuery TestQuery("SELECT ename,empno,job,hiredate from
             EMP",&TestConn);
    TestQuery.Execute();
    DBColString colEname(&TestQuery, 1);
    DBColNumber colEmpno(&TestQuery, 2);
    DBColString colJob(&TestQuery, 3);
    DBColDate colHiredate(&TestQuery, 4);
    while(TestQuery.MoveNext())
    {
    cout    << "EName:  " << colEname << endl
            << "Empno:  " << colEmpno  << endl
        << "Job:    " << colJob    << endl
        << "Hired   " << colHiredate << endl << endl;
    }
}
```

Example 1: *Typical C++ app.*

This might include more operators and perhaps more advanced date manipulation.

Since most member functions are declared virtual, new column classes can be inherited from existing implementations. This technique can be used to add or modify behavior. For example, to change the way a column type prints its output, override the *PrintValue()* member function.

The *DBObject* class currently contains member functions to let derived classes set and get errors. A possible extension would be to throw an exception after the error message is copied into the buffer. Another extension could have the *SetError()* function terminate the application if the error were severe. Because all errors are processed in the *DBObject* class, your error-handling strategy can be implemented in this class.

Conclusion

Class libraries like DBObjects will play a substantial role in reducing complexity and enhancing interoperability between the C++ language and relational-database technology. The benefits don't just end here, however. By-products of our approach are portability, efficient database access at low cost, and reduced maintenance. Who knows? This type of technology may even aid a migration from RDBMS to the great nirvana of OODBMS.

```
ENAME  EMPNO JOB       HIREDATE     ENAME  EMPNO JOB       HIREDATE
-----  ----- ---       --------     -----  ----- ---       --------
SMITH  7369  CLERK     17-DEC-80    CLARK  7782  MANAGER   09-JUN-81
ALLEN  7499  SALESMAN  20-FEB-81    SCOTT  7788  ANALYST   09-DEC-82
WARD   7521  SALESMAN  22-FEB-81    KING   7839  PRESIDENT 17-NOV-81
JONES  7566  MANAGER   02-APR-81    TURNER 7844  SALESMAN  08-SEP-81
MARTIN 7654  SALESMAN  28-SEP-81    ADAMS  7876  CLERK     12-JAN-83
BLAKE  7698  MANAGER   01-MAY-81    JAMES  7900  CLERK     03-DEC-81
```

Example 2: ***Contents of EMP table.***

```
EName:  SMITH
Empno:  7369
Job:    CLERK
Hired   17-DEC-1980 00:00:00
EName:  ALLEN
Empno:  7499
Job:    SALESMAN
Hired   20-FEB-1981 00:00:00
EName:  WARD
Empno:  7521
Job:    SALESMAN
Hired   22-FEB-1981 00:00:00
EName:  JONES
Empno:  7566
Job:    MANAGER
Hired   02-APR-1981 00:00:00
EName:  MARTIN
Empno:  7654
Job:    SALESMAN
Hired   28-SEP-1981 00:00:00
EName:  BLAKE
Empno:  7698
Job:    MANAGER
Hired   01-MAY-1981 00:00:00
EName:  CLARK
Empno:  7782
Job:    MANAGER
Hired   09-JUN-1981 00:00:00
EName:  SCOTT
Empno:  7788
Job:    ANALYST
Hired   09-DEC-1982 00:00:00
EName:  KING
Empno:  7839
Job:    PRESIDENT
Hired   17-NOV-1981 00:00:00
EName:  TURNER
Empno:  7844
Job:    SALESMAN
Hired   08-SEP-1981 00:00:00
EName:  ADAMS
Empno:  7876
Job:    CLERK
Hired   12-JAN-1983 00:00:00
EName:  JAMES
Empno:  7900
Job:    CLERK
Hired   03-DEC-1981 00:00:00
```

Example 3: *Output generated by Example 1.*

Listing One

```
////////////////////////////////////////////////////////////////////////
//  DBConnection Implementation
////////////////////////////////////////////////////////////////////////
#include <dbobject.h>
// Default Constructor
DBConnection::DBConnection()
{
   m_pLoginCursor = 0;
   Reset();
}
// Constructor with access string
DBConnection::DBConnection(const char *AccessString)
{
   m_pLoginCursor = 0;
   Connect(AccessString);
}
DBConnection::~DBConnection()
{
  if (IsConnected()) {
     Disconnect();
  }
  delete m_pLoginCursor;
}
short DBConnection::Disconnect()
{
  if (IsConnected()) {
      if (ologof(m_pLoginCursor)) {
         SetDBError(m_pLoginCursor->csrarc,DBErrorMsg(m_pLoginCursor->csrrc));
         SetError(-210, m_pUserName);
     return 0;
      }
      else {
         Reset();
         m_nIsConnected = 0;
         return 1;
      }
  }
  else {
     SetError(-203, NOLOGIN_CURSOR );
     return 0;
  }
}
short DBConnection::Connect(const char *pAccess)
{
    if (! m_pLoginCursor) {
       m_pLoginCursor = new DBOBJLOGIN;
       if (!m_pLoginCursor) {
          SetError(-100, ALLOCATION_ERROR);
          return 0;
       }
    }
    if (!*pAccess) {
```

```
        SetError(-200, NULLACCESSS_STRING);
        return 0;
    }
    char *pPassWrd = strchr(pAccess, '/');
    if (!pPassWrd) {
        SetError(-201, NOPASSWORD);
        return 0;
    }
    pPassWrd++; // past the '/'
    int  UserLen = strlen(pAccess) - strlen(pPassWrd);
    char User[30];
    if (UserLen > 30) UserLen = 30; // truncate
    strncpy(User, pAccess, UserLen-1 );
    User[UserLen-1] = 0;

    // Copy to member
    strcpy(m_pUserName, User);
    if (orlon(m_pLoginCursor, hda, (char*)pAccess)) {
        SetDBError(m_pLoginCursor->csrarc, DBErrorMsg(m_pLoginCursor->csrrc) );
        SetError(-205, m_pUserName);
        return 0;
    }
    Reset();
    m_nIsConnected = 1;
    return 1;
}
short DBConnection::Commit()
{
    if (m_pLoginCursor) {
        if (ocom(m_pLoginCursor)) {
      SetDBError(m_pLoginCursor->csrarc,DBErrorMsg(m_pLoginCursor->csrrc));
            SetError(-206, m_pUserName);
            return 0;
        }
        Reset();
        return 1;
     }
     else {
      SetDBError(m_pLoginCursor->csrarc,DBErrorMsg(m_pLoginCursor->csrrc));
            SetError(-202, m_pUserName);
     }
     Reset();
     return 1;
}
short DBConnection::SetAutoCommit(short OnOrOff)
{
   if (m_pLoginCursor) {
      if (OnOrOff == 1) {
         if (ocon(m_pLoginCursor)) {
      SetDBError(m_pLoginCursor->csrarc,DBErrorMsg(m_pLoginCursor->csrrc));
            SetError(-206, m_pUserName);
            return 0;
         }
         else {
```

```
            Reset();
            return 1;
         }
      }
      else {
         if (ocof(m_pLoginCursor)) {
      SetDBError(m_pLoginCursor->csrarc,DBErrorMsg(m_pLoginCursor->csrrc));
          SetError(-206, m_pUserName);
          return 0;
         }
         else {
           Reset();
           return 1;
         }
      }
   }
   else {
      SetDBError(m_pLoginCursor->csrarc, DBErrorMsg(m_pLoginCursor->csrrc) );
      SetError(201, "No Oracle Login Object Defined");
      return 0;
   }
}
short DBConnection::Rollback()
{
   if (m_pLoginCursor) {
      if (orol(m_pLoginCursor)) {
      SetDBError(m_pLoginCursor->csrarc,DBErrorMsg(m_pLoginCursor->csrrc));
          SetError(-206, m_pUserName);
          return 0;
      }
      else {
          Reset();
          return 1;
      }
   }
   else {
      SetDBError(m_pLoginCursor->csrarc, DBErrorMsg(m_pLoginCursor->csrrc));
      SetError(201, NOLOGIN_CURSOR);
      return 0;
   }
}
const char* DBConnection::DBErrorMsg(int ErrorNo)
{
    if (m_pLoginCursor) {
       static char ExceptionBuffer[MAX_DBMSG];
       memset(ExceptionBuffer,0, MAX_DBMSG);
       oerhms(m_pLoginCursor, ErrorNo, ExceptionBuffer, MAX_DBMSG-1);
       return ExceptionBuffer;
    }
    else {
       SetError(-203, NOLOGIN_CURSOR);
       return "";
    }
}
```

Performance Testing, ODBC, and Native SQL APIs

Ken North

Performance is a major factor in the selection and tuning of almost all client/server application components—the network, server, database design, and even the SQL API. Application performance can be affected by network latency, programming techniques, and client libraries, among other factors. To objectively evaluate an SQL API, you must differentiate between application performance and API performance. You must also use a vehicle for performance testing that isolates the API as a variable while holding constant other factors that affect performance. APIBench, the benchmark software

---

Ken, a consultant and developer, is author of Windows Multi-DBMS Programming *(John Wiley & Sons, 1995). He can be contacted at 71301.1306@compuserve.com. Reprinted courtesy of* Dr. Dobb's Sourcebook.

described in this article, lets you vary the API while executing identical queries using the same data, network libraries, and other C/S components.

Most SQL engines and servers let developers use more than one API. SQL DBMSs traditionally include a native or proprietary interface that is either a call level interface (CLI) or embedded SQL (ESQL). More recently, developers have had the option of writing to the Open Database Connectivity (ODBC) API. ODBC provides a single interface for SQL queries to access a variety of relational and nonrelational databases. A typical client/server database architecture puts the database engine and the data on a server machine that is physically separate from and networked to its clients. ODBC operates in this two-tier architecture by putting the Driver Manager and one or more database drivers on the machine with the client application. ODBC drivers are DLLs for Windows and OS/2, and shared libraries for UNIX and the Macintosh. The ODBC Driver Manager fields an application's ODBC function calls and routes them, when necessary, to the appropriate driver.

C/S Benchmark Architecture

APIBench is a Windows client that uses an executable program for its user interface and five DLLs to interface to different database APIs. The benchmark software's extensible architecture lets you plug in other APIs by developing DLLs and updating configuration files. Figure 1 illustrates the architecture of APIBench. The DLLs that contain the native and ODBC code have a common skeleton, so each type of test has comparable functions. For example, all of the DLLs include a *doInsert* function to perform the INSERT test, *printTime* to update the log, and so on.

My focus with APIBench has been client/server performance testing. The network layer for these tests has used different network libraries because the software works with a variety of protocols and networking components. The latter are components that operate over lower-level network protocols, such as TCP/IP, IPX/SPX, and NetBIOS. Examples include Oracle's SQL*Net and Transparent Network Substrate (TNS), and SQL Server's Tabular Data Stream (TDS). The layered architecture means that TNS and TDS can operate with various network protocols and a client application can treat the network layer as an abstraction. Changes in the network layer may affect performance and, by extension, the results of the SQL API benchmarks. (Such changes don't affect the native or ODBC code in these programs.) In other words, the Oracle benchmark DLL will run without modification on Windows clients using combinations such as SQL*Net with NetWare and IPX/SPX or Windows/NT with TCP/IP. The network libraries are mostly transparent to the client application. With the exception of changing TDS packet size for SQL Server, there is no logic in the SQL API that varies based on the underlying network libraries.

The test suite includes typical SQL operations using an employee table and a department table. When operating against them, the program uses an index on the employee ID and department ID, respectively. The tests include an

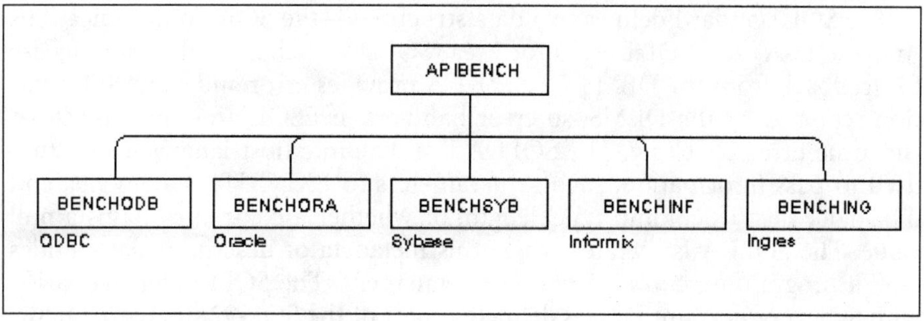

Figure 1: *SQL API benchmark program (APIBench) and dynamic link libraries.*

INSERT test to populate both tables, two UPDATE and two DELETE tests, and five query (SELECT) tests. The SQL statements for the five SELECT tests use joins, aggregate functions, WHERE filters, and individual row selections. The test suite uses a mix of prepare and execute queries and direct-execution queries. A prepared query, sometimes called a "compiled query," is typically faster for repetitive operations, while direct-execution queries are preferable for one-time execution of an SQL statement.

The benchmark software creates two log files with individual test information and an array of execution times. The individual ODBC and native DLLs execute one or more of the SQL queries defined in SQLSTMTS.H, measure the time to execute each statement, and record information about the test in BENCH.OUT; see Listing One. The programs also write the execution time for each test to RESULT.OUT. Before relying on the accuracy of the numbers in RESULT.OUT, one should check BENCH.OUT for anomalies such as execution errors, status messages, or incorrect row counts.

SQL Programming and Embedded SQL

ANSI and ISO recently approved a new standard for an SQL CLI, but the benchmark DLLs described here used older SQL APIs. The Sybase System 10 and Oracle 7 DLLs use a CLI to access their data while the CA Open-Ingres and Informix 5 DLLs use ESQL. The CLIs support run-time binding to data, while ESQL represents compile-time binding because it requires preprocessing and compilation. SQL products that support ESQL typically provide preprocessors for common languages such as C, Cobol, and Fortran. The preprocessor scans the source code and replaces embedded SQL statements with calls to modules in a vendor-supplied object library. A programmer compiles and links the preprocessor output and must repeat the process when there are revisions to the source or database design. The Oracle Pro*C preprocessor supports ESQL for C programs. It lets you create a native DLL for Oracle that uses ESQL to complement the benchmark DLL that uses the Oracle Call Interface (OCI).

The SQL standard defines two data structures—the SQL Communications Area (SQLCA) and SQL Descriptor Area (SQLDA)—that ESQL programs use for feedback from the DBMS. The SQLCA provides error and status information reported by the DBMS, so error handlers in ESQL programs use it for run-time error checking. The SQLDA is a dynamic host-language structure used to pass information, such as parameters to EXECUTE statements, and metadata, such as column type, length, or whether a column contains a null value. The SQLDA is the area where this metadata or descriptor data resides after a program executes a DESCRIBE statement. The SQLDA format varied with SQL products until it was defined as part of the SQL-92 standard. ODBC 3.0 will be the first release of ODBC that uses this type of descriptor.

Embedded statements in these benchmark programs don't include hard-coded column names. Instead, they use ESQL's DESCRIBE statement, dynamic SQL, and the SQLDA.

Typical SQL software includes a query optimizer that processes SQL statements to determine the optimum access path or the execution plan for a query. Many SQL tools permit you to prepare or compile statements that will be used repetitively by saving the query's execution plan. PREPARE checks the validity of a statement including dynamic parameters and optimizes its execution. An application submits the prepare request once and may then use multiple execution requests. This speeds up processing for repetitive queries. For single-statement execution, ESQL provides EXECUTE IMMEDIATE to avoid the overhead of preparing a statement.

The logic to execute dynamic SELECT statements illustrates the use of these features. ESQL uses host variables from the host programming language in SQL statements. ESQL programmers use BEGIN DECLARE SECTION and END DECLARE SECTION to frame the declaration of host variables. The routine described here declares a host variable for a dynamically defined SQL string and uses it when preparing the SELECT statement *EXEC SQL PREPARE sel_stmt FROM :SQLstring;*. The dynamic SELECT routine declares host variables, writes the SQL statement to the log file, and then starts the timer for the benchmark test. It allocates an SQLDA, declares a cursor for the query, and prepares the SELECT statement. Next, the routine DESCRIBEs the statement into a query descriptor and executes a loop that sets variables (*data type, length*) based on the column descriptions. The loop also aggregates the cursor size using the length of each column. After stepping through all columns, the routine allocates a data buffer based on the cursor size, adjusts for null indicators, and opens the query cursor. Then it executes a FETCH loop using the query descriptor and closes the cursor. Finally, it stops the benchmark timer, updates benchmark log files, and frees the data buffers.

Native CLIs and ODBC

The Sybase Open Client (CT-Library) and Oracle Call Interface (OCI) do not use source-code preprocessing because they support run-time calls to a library of data-access functions. The CT-Library is new with System 10. It is a successor to DB-Library and includes support for System-10 features such as cursors. It is also intended to operate with servers other than SQL Server so it includes functions such as *ct_capability* to define the features available with a specific connection. OCI includes connection functions, binding functions, statement processing, transaction control, and results processing that includes array fetches. It supports cursors and batched execution of SQL statements. To process a typical SQL query when using a CLI, you create a connection to the database, bind the columns in the query to buffers or memory variables in the application, submit the SQL command for processing, and use a loop to fetch the results from the query. CLIs such as ODBC and CT-Library include functions that provide a counterpart to ESQL's immediate execution and prepared execution of queries.

Several features of ODBC programming are relevant to this benchmark program. Because ODBC is a CLI, there is no source-code preprocessing: ODBC includes functions to connect to databases, prepare and submit SQL statements, and so on. Unlike other CLIs, however, ODBC can operate on multiple databases by loading the appropriate database driver at run time. ODBC uses handles to track resources such as memory and errors associated with the application environment, connections, and SQL statements. It includes functions that return information about the API and SQL dialect that a driver implements. ODBC operates on data using SQL statements, so it includes functions for both direct and prepared query execution. PREPAREand EXECUTE queries permit the DBMS to optimize the query, store its access plan, and use the plan repetitively without repeating the optimization process. ODBC's *SQLExecDirect* is the counterpart to ESQL's EXECUTE IMMEDIATE, while *SQLPrepare* and *SQLExecute* are the counterparts to PREPARE and EXECUTE, respectively. ODBC drivers sometimes emulate prepared queries when a DBMS does not natively support them. For example, the driver for Microsoft SQL Server will create temporary stored procedures to use when an ODBC application uses prepared queries.

A program using ODBC must allocate the environment handle before other handles, so BENCHODB, the DLL for ODBC testing, allocates an environment handle in its *LibMain* routine. A description of the ODBC equivalent to the ESQL dynamic SELECT routine may provide a better understanding of CLI programming. BENCHODB's *doSelect* routine processes SELECT queries using prepare and execute logic. It writes the statement to the log file, allocates a statement handle, and starts the benchmark timer. The program prepares the query using *SQLPrepare* and then calls *SQLNumResultCols* to get the number of columns in the result-set buffer. Next, it uses a loop to describe each column with *SQLDescribeCol* so that it can allocate storage for database columns. To bind columns to memory variables, *doSelect* calls *SQLBindCol* and passes arguments such as the column type and length. After binding columns, it calls *SQLExecute* to execute the statement and then executes a fetch loop that steps through the result set by calling *SQLFetch*. Each call to *SQLFetch* populates the bound columns with new data from the database.

Once the program completes the fetch loop, it stops the benchmark timer and updates the benchmark logs.

Some of the benchmark code for ODBC logic reflects the fact that ODBC supports both escape clauses and parameter markers in SQL statements. The *SQLBindParameter* function binds a buffer to a parameter marker. ODBC drivers support the use of escape clauses to delineate SQL extensions such as outer joins, LIKE predicates, and procedure calls. Using these escape clauses simplifies the writing of interoperable SQL, but bypassing the scan for escape clauses may increase performance in some circumstances. Some of the SQL statements used with APIBench are in two forms.

ESQL and CLI Differences

To provide a realistic basis for comparison, the APIBench software uses techniques representative of typical ESQL and CLI coding. This guarantees that you will see differences as you examine the source code for each DLL. Whether using ESQL or a native CLI, developing native code is different from ODBC programming in several respects. The native programmer targets just one DBMS, the features, function calls, and data types of which are known. ODBC programmers write multi-DBMS code to get information about the database and the driver so that an application can adapt to the available features and types at run time. Error-handling differences arise in part because CLIs don't use an SQLCA for run-time error checking. ESQL programmers sometimes

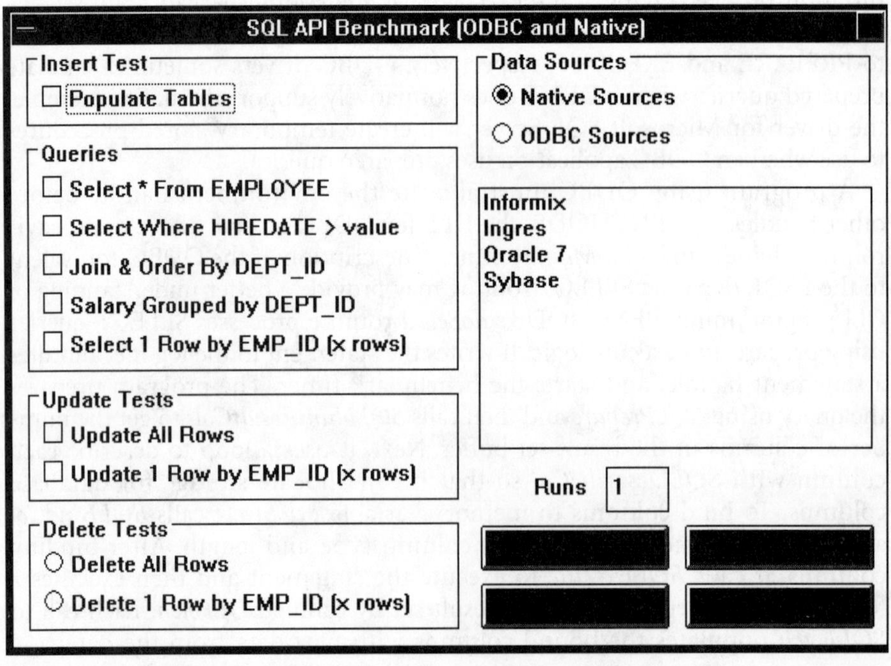

Figure 2: *The APIBench form to select SQL APIs and benchmark.*

use a WHENEVER clause to define error-handling logic that will be executed whenever certain errors occur, but developers using a CLI such as ODBC usually test the return code from each function for errors. To retrieve error information after calling ODBC functions, developers use a loop that calls *SQLError* to retrieve all of the error codes and messages for a specific function. CLIs bind columns instead of using ESQL host variables. *SQLBindCol* is the ODBC equivalent of ESQL's host variables, while CT-Library uses *ct_bind.*

ODBC differs from ESQL and other CLIs in that it is multidatabase and therefore includes functions to get run-time information about the database and driver it is using. APIBench includes a few examples of the use of adaptive techniques in ODBC programs. The source code for BENCHODB uses *SQLGetInfo*, an ODBC information function that returns the driver's version number. With version 1.0 drivers, the program uses *SQLSetParam* calls to specify values to replace parameter markers. *SQLSetParam* is a function replaced by 2.0's *SQLBindParameter,* so the program calls *SQLBindParameter* to bind parameters if the driver is a version 2 driver.

Details such as the handling of buffers for column data and the functions to describe those columns vary with APIs. The ODBC code binds columns in the database to memory variables by calling *SQLBindCol,* gets type information from *SQLGetTypeInfo,* and uses *SQLDescribe* to describe columns in result sets. An ESQL application uses known data types and a DESCRIBE statement to get descriptor data that includes null indicators, length, and type. ODBC 3.0 implements additional function calls to get descriptors similar to SQL-92 descriptors, so the logic of the ODBC benchmark DLL testing may change in the future.

Performance-Testing Considerations

When creating the benchmark DLLs, it is important to properly frame the individual tests with function calls to get timing information. To add new DLLs, you can use the placement of *_ftime (&begin)* and *_ftime (&end)* calls in an existing native DLL as a model. To verify the accuracy of the times reported in RESULT.OUT, examine the details of each test recorded in BENCH.OUT. The results of individual tests should be as expected and consistent with tests using other native APIs and ODBC. For example, if you specify a row count of 2500, verify that the log shows that the program populated the tables with 2500 rows and that subsequent tests use 2500 row tables. A simple oversight such as running the populate test twice in sequence, without a deletion test, will populate the table with double the expected number of rows and skew the data from subsequent tests. Other factors may influence results. By setting *NativeSQL=Yes* in BENCHMRK.INI, you can enable logic in the ODBC benchmark DLL to use native SQL by foregoing the use of ODBC escape clauses.

Although the goal of these benchmark programs is to provide the best "apples-to-apples" comparison between ODBC and other APIs, in some areas, comparisons are inherently problematic. For instance, Microsoft and SQL

Server use a Tabular Data Stream (TDS) protocol to send data to and from the server. TDS uses a variable packet size with a default of 512 bytes. ODBC defines a connection option (*SQLConnectOption*) to vary the packet size for Microsoft's SQL Server driver. Intersolv lets you modify the packet size by using a switch in ODBC.INI. To test with different packet sizes, revise the Sybase CT-Library benchmark code to negotiate packet size with the server.

When running these tests using Intersolv DataDirect drivers, ODBC execution times were often less than native times, sometimes dramatically so. Two of the reasons appear to be the skill level of the driver developer and the types of performance optimizations—enabled by a switch in the ODBC.INI file—available with each new generation of ODBC drivers.

My testing of one Ingres query produced results that provided an excellent example of the effect of the .INI settings. If I used recommended driver settings, the ODBC code executed in about half of the time required for my native code. The driver was a prerelease version from Intersolv, so I contacted the company for information about the optimizations available through various ODBC.INI settings. The driver developer described settings that affected cache size and other optimizations. With that explanation, I could disable those optimizations and produce ODBC test times virtually identical to my native tests. However, most people are likely to read the documentation and use the correct switch settings, making the apples-to-apples comparison that enables the driver's performance features.

Building and Operating APIBench

To implement new native API tests, you create a DLL containing the native code and update the benchmark program's initialization file (see BENCHMRK.INI, Listing Two). To update BENCHMRK.INI, add to the list of DLLs (API_DLLS) and a section for API that includes the name of the new DLL.

The C source code for the executable and DLLs (available electronically on the diskette) has been compiled and tested using Microsoft Visual C++. The programs that do not use ESQL are not preprocessed. They contain conditionals, so you can build them using Borland C++. For example, the source uses an *#ifdef* block because Borland uses a *timeb* structure, whereas the Microsoft compiler uses a *_timeb* structure. I prefer C++ over C, but C still enjoys an advantage when porting to multiple platforms. ODBC is available with Windows, Windows NT, Windows 95, OS/2, Macintosh System 7, and various flavors of UNIX such as AIX and Solaris. The MAKE files and IDE files that accompany this software are for the Windows version only.

The benchmark application uses a simple form interface, as in Figure 2. To run the benchmarks, select the individual tests with a check box, an API push button (native or ODBC), a data source, and finally, the Run command button. The application also presents buttons to create tables, clear prior selections, and exit the application. Because network latency and database checkpointing can affect the execution time for an individual run, you will get more reliable data by executing multiple runs and calculating mean execution times. The benchmark form includes a control that permits you to enter the number of times to run the selected tests. My APIBench tests with four native APIs have shown that there is no performance degradation when using ODBC.

Listing One

```
Native Sybase
Date and time: 7-6-1995  15:19:52.21

    TDS Packet Size: 512

INSERT INTO EMPLOYEE
    (FIRST_NAME, MID_NAME, LAST_NAME, EMP_ID, DEPT_ID, SALARY, HIRE_DATE)
    VALUES (?,?,?,?,?,?,?)
Prepare & (Execute x 2500)                        98.15

CT_Library: row select (prepare and execute)

SELECT *
    FROM EMPLOYEE
    WHERE EMP_ID = ?

<doRowSelect> ct_dynamic success following ct_param

<doRowSelect> ct_send success following ct_param
Prepare & (Execute * 1)                      153.46

==============================
ODBC System10 07
Date and time: 7-6-1995  15:31:09.93  Driver ODBC Version: 02.10
                                                        Native SQL: Yes
SELECT *
    FROM EMPLOYEE
    WHERE EMP_ID = ?
Prepare & (Execute * 2500)                        264.53
==============================
```

Listing Two

```
[API]
API_DLLS = INFORMIX,ORACLE7,Sybase,INGRES

[INFORMIX]
Description="Informix"
DLL="BENCHINF.DLL"
```

```
LOGIN="test"
PWD="test"

RowCount=2500

[ODBC]
RowCount=2500

[ORACLE7]
Description="Oracle 7"
DLL="BENCHOR7.DLL"
LOGIN="test1@x:training"
PWD="test"
RowCount=2500

[INGRES]
Description="Ingres"
DLL="BENCHING.DLL"
RowCount=2500

[Sybase]
Description="Sybase"
DLL="BENCHSYB.DLL"
RowCount=2500
```

End Listings

Object Persistence with Relational Databases

Chuck Allison

"Companies without a strategy for client/server are creating the next generation of legacy systems." [1] Those are strong words for today's developers who are peddling as fast as they can to keep up with the pace of our industry. Client/server (C/S) computing can indeed be a formidable challenge, but it is one that developers must face and master to be productive and competitive in the long term. Fortunately for this journal's audience, object-

---

Chuck Allison is a former columnist with CUJ and a Senior Software Engineer in the Information and Communication Systems Department of the Church of Jesus Christ of Latter Day Saints in Salt Lake City. He has a B.S. and M.S. in mathematics, has been programming since 1975, and has been teaching and developing in C since 1984. His current interest is object-oriented technology and education. He is a member of X3J16, the ANSI C++ Standards Committee. Chuck can be reached on the Internet at 72640.1507@compuserve.com. *Reprinted courtesy of* C/C++ Users Journal.

oriented (OO) technology, and C++ in particular, play a key role in C/S solutions.

In this article I present a simple C++ class framework for object persistence that can work with any SQL-conforming relational database, in either a standalone or C/S environment.

Client/Server Architecture

Client/Server concepts have evolved in part from a key insight of the structured development era — the separation of interface and implementation, which has also provided the basis for the current revolution in object-orientation. This high degree of modularity enables a "building block" approach that results in systems and components that are flexible, reusable, reliable, and efficient.

A typical C/S environment has three main categories of services (see Figure 1):

- *User services* display information and gather data from an end user, and call upon the functionality of other services to support the user in the execution of business processes.
- A *business service* is responsible for making decisions based on available information and business rules in order to perform a set of functions. It is responsible for generating usable information and building the logic to request data from data services.
- A business service relies upon *data services* and other business services to help perform its service. The data services layer provides controlled access to information stored in corporate databases.

Separating systems into these three layers has a number of benefits. First, a logically-layered architecture allows an orderly division of labor that optimizes the use of technical resources. Data services personnel are typically DBAs, experts in both the conceptual and physical aspects of the corporate DBMS. Business services developers create reusable components without any concern for user interface issues. User services personnel call upon business services without any direct knowledge of the data services layer.

In short, distinct teams can do what they do well, with results that fit together. Secondly, the number of opportunities for reuse increases. By developing modular components, new applications can plug into existing services, or can extend those services with a minimum of effort. Modular components also promote maintainability and distributivity. Each service resides in a unique component, providing a single point of update for manageable evolution. Service components can be deployed on a single server and shared by all clients in a way that optimizes network performance.

Traditional corporate information-systems (IS) solutions have been anchored in data modeling. This has caused undue emphasis on data structures and database models too early in the development cycle. Object modeling, on the other hand, encourages a service-based approach, allowing designers to focus on the responsibilities of business objects, and to leave physical data issues to implementers. In an object-centered architecture, developers and users alike focus on the business, and user services and data services exist merely to display and store business objects (see Figure 2). It is usually much easier to get all the parties involved to agree on functionality than on schema and data type concerns.

Distributed Computing

From the perspective of modularity, this three-tier architecture is beneficial whether or not you deploy the different layers on separate platforms. Three logical tiers can exist on a single machine, or you can physically distribute them across distinct client machines, application servers, and data servers. In our environment, we use Visual BASIC for presentation on client machines, Visual C++ to implement business objects on application servers, and Oracle on data servers to provide object persistence. Our client machines still run 16-bit Windows, while the application servers operate under Windows NT 3.51, and the Oracle databases reside on VAXes running OpenVMS.

Two very critical architectural issues immediately present themselves:

1. How to connect the different layers efficiently across networks, and
2. How to store objects in a relational database.

Being mainly a Microsoft shop, we use Microsoft's connectivity solutions: OLE and ODBC (see Figure 3). Remote OLE Automation provides client applications concurrent access to business objects in a networked environment. The ODBC standard resolves connectivity issues between applications and relational databases.

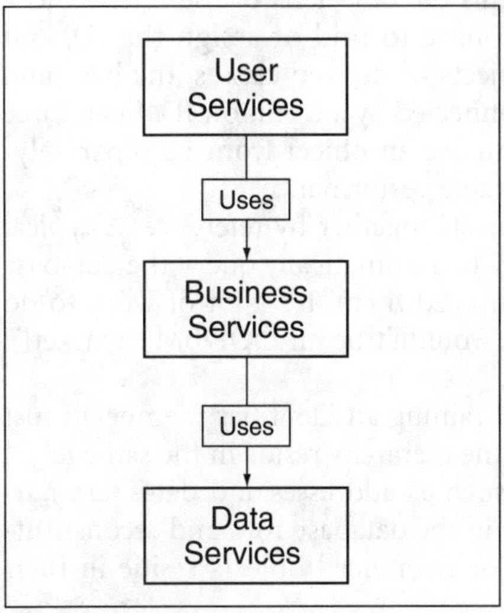

Figure 1: *Typical C/S service.*

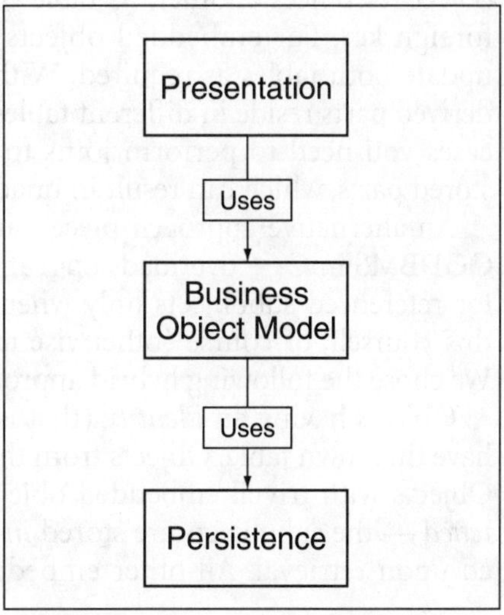

Figure 2: *A three-tired object model.*

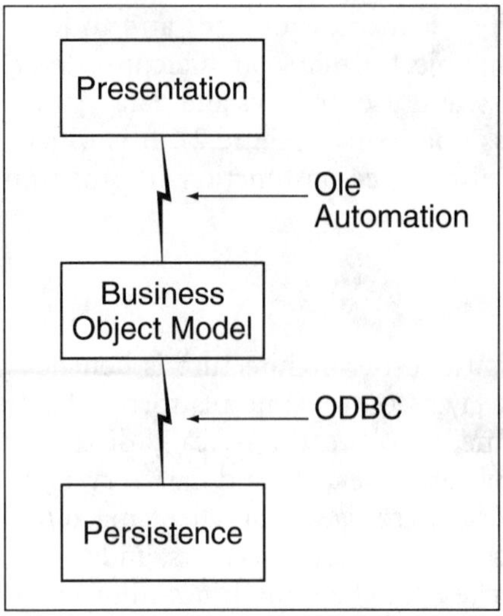

Figure 3: *Connecting layers in a three-tier system.*

Mapping Objects to Tables

Persistence is unquestionably the struggling step-child of the OO revolution. Object concepts have been around since 1967, Smalltalk and C++ were under development almost 20 years ago, and methodologies have now evolved to the point that anyone not doing objects is just not "with it." When it comes to object persistence, however, most of the corporate world is definitely not "with it," and for good reason.

Not to say that robust object-oriented database management systems aren't available. There are a number of powerful OODBMSs that provide persistent storage of objects with a minimum of fuss. Typically, an OODBMS reads existing class specifications and arranges for retrieval and update of objects with little or no programmer intervention. But the complexity of corporate information systems as a rule stretches a DBMS to its limits, and OODBMSs have not yet gained wide acceptance in a corporate environment. Even if they had, the expense of converting corporate data services guarantees that relational systems will be the norm for some time to come.

Since a relational DBMS stores information in two-dimensional tables, it is necessary to map objects attributes to fit the relational model. The academic approach is to store objects of each class in a table unique to that class. If an object references another, its table contains the object ID of the referent as a foreign key. For embedded objects you have to find or assign the ID, and update both tables as required. With objects of derived classes, the base and derived parts reside in different tables, connected by a common ID. In all three cases you need to perform joins to compose an object from its separately-stored parts, which can result in unacceptable performance.

An alternative approach pieces subobjects together by reference. A typical OODBMS in C++ overloads `operator->` to automatically query the database for referenced subobjects only when you need them. It's a lot of work to do this yourself, of course (otherwise there wouldn't be an OODBMS market!). We chose the following hybrid approach:

Objects having an *identity* (that is, containing an identifier member) must have their own table. Objects from the same hierarchy reside in the same table. Objects with trivial embedded objects, such as addresses and dates, are *flattened* — the subobjects are stored *in situ* in the database row, and reconstituted upon retrieval. All other embedded or referenced objects reside in their

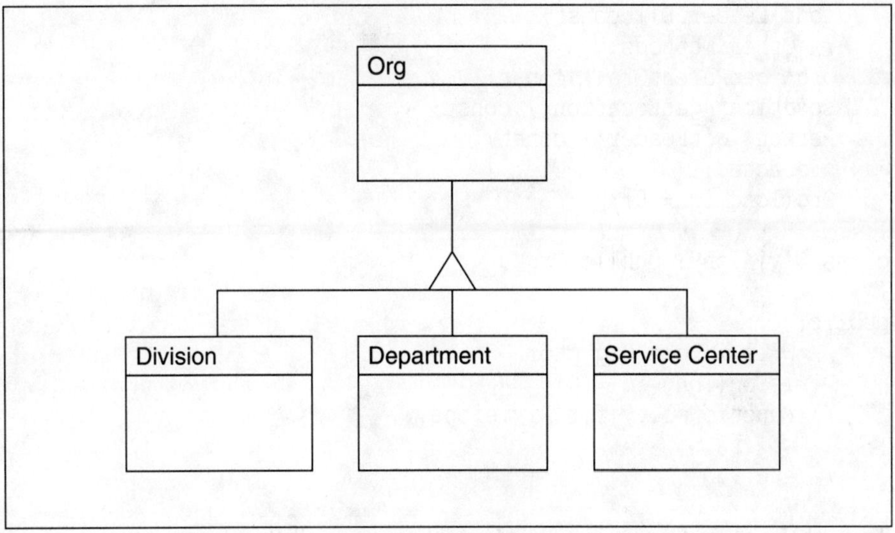

Figure 4: ***Typical organization hierarchy.***

own tables and are accessed through simple pointers returned by member functions (with names like `getParentOrg`).

Our derived objects usually add functionality without adding extra attributes, so storing a hierarchy in a single table isn't as space-wasteful as it might seem at first blush. Coupled with Oracle's variable-length storage scheme, it's a non issue. To make this work, it is necessary to have a field in the table that indicates the type of object the row represents. As an example, Figure 4 depicts a simple hierarchy of organization types. The corresponding SQL columns might include some of the following:

```
ObjectID  TypeID  Name  LocationID  LeaderID
```

The C++ class definitions might then look like this:

```
class Org
{
    // Record attributes:
    long ObjectID;
    long TypeID;
    CString Name;
    long LocationID;
    long LeaderID;
public:
    // Accessors:
    long getObjectID() const;
    long getTypeID() const;
    CString getName() const;
    long LocationID() const;
```

```
    long LeaderID() const;
    // Other methods:
    Org* getParentOrg() const;
    Location* getLocation() const;
    Person* getLeader() const;
    protected:
    Org(long id = 0);
};
class Division : public Org
{
public:
    // Will invoke Org ctor
    Division(long id = 0);
    // Functionality for Divisions...
};
    // etc...
```

To find the parent organization of another, you call the appropriate method and get a pointer back:

```
// Retrieve an Org by ID
Org myOrg(1234);
Org* myParent =
    myOrg.getParentOrg();
// Use parent object
cout << myParent.getName();
// Must delete referents explicitly
delete myParent;
```

The Open Database Connectivity specification (ODBC) manages database access through a connection. A connection string contains all the information necessary to identify and log on to a network database. Through the connection a program can execute any SQL statement and retrieve query results.

The Microsoft Foundation Class library (MFC) that accompanies Visual C++ encapsulates a connection in the `CDatabase` class. A `CRecordset` object provides the functions you would expect to traverse a query result set and update records. Visual C++'s Class Wizard creates custom recordset classes for you directly from pre-defined ODBC datasets. Listing 1 shows the header file generated for a projection of the `Employees` table in the North Wind sample database distributed with Microsoft Access, as shown in Table 1 (I've left out some fields to save print space). Listing 2 has the implementation file, and a test program is in Listing 3.

A Persistence Framework for C++

A business object class like `Org` needs to shield you from the details of DBMS access. It also needs to shield itself from the fickle forces of the class library

Employee ID	Last Name	First Name	Home Phone	Reports To
1	Davolio	Nancy	(206) 555-9857	2
2	Fuller	Andrew	(206) 555-9482	
3	Leverling	Janice	(206) 555-3412	2
4	Peacock	Phyllis	(206) 555-8122	2
5	Buchanan	B. L.	(71) 555-4848	2
6	Suyama	Michael	(71) 555-7733	5
7	King	Jonathan	(71) 555-5598	5
8	Callahan	Linda	(206) 555-1189	2
9	Dodsworth	Annabella	(71) 555-4444	5

Table 1: *The table that generated the header file in listing 1.*

industry. Instead of depending directly on MFC, it is better to have a layer of abstraction between the business object model and the DBMS access mechanism. This way the business services layer doesn't have to change should you replace MFC with another library.

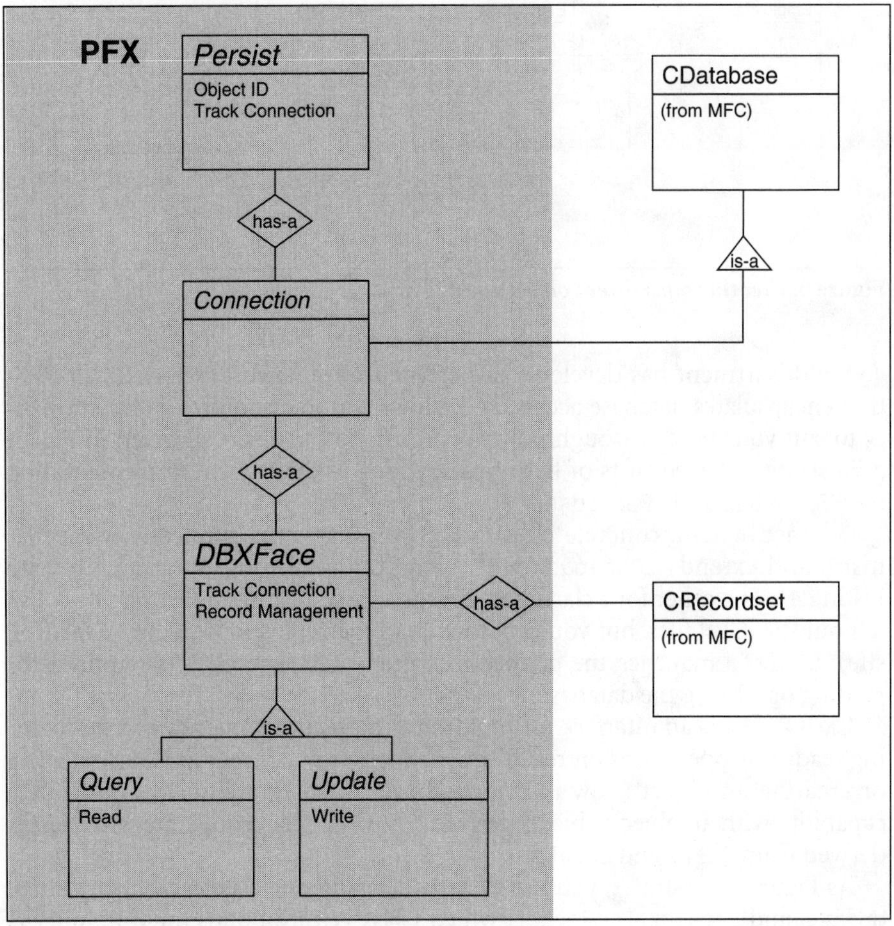

Figure 5: *PFX persistence framework.*

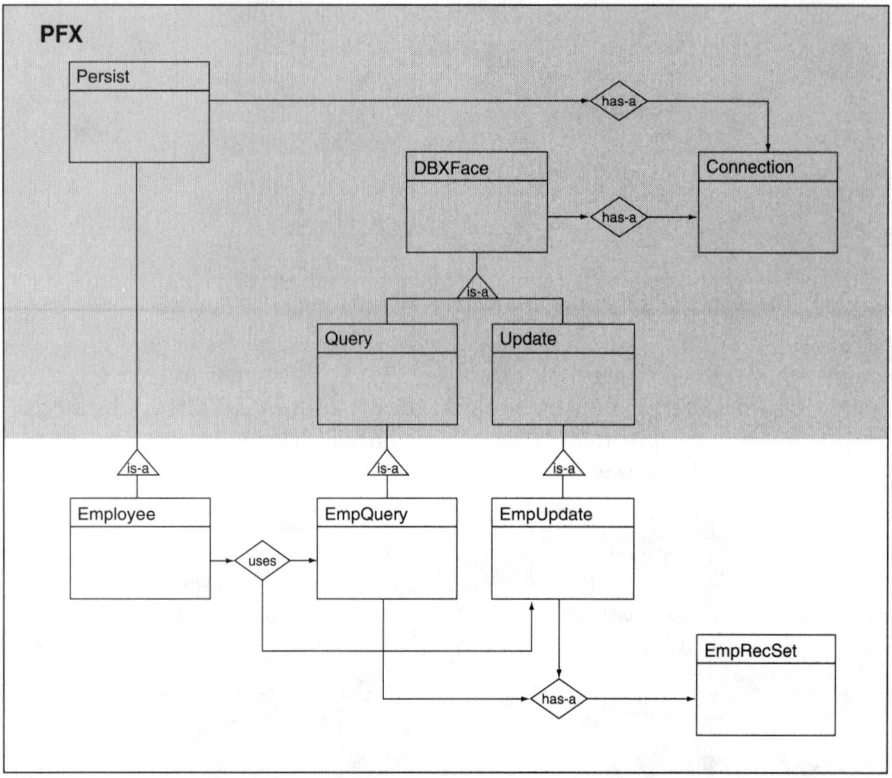

Figure 6: ***Creating a persistent object with PFX.***

My department has developed a persistence framework, which I call PFX, that encapsulates database access, and allows you to customize its functionality to suit your needs through polymorphism. As the object diagram in Figure 5 illustrates, PFX consists of five classes, which in the current implementation use `CDatabase` and `CRecordset`.

`Connection` is a concrete class that encapsulates the connectivity mechanism, and extends `CDatabase` with some housekeeping functionality (see Listing 4). The other four classes are abstract. (See Listings 5 through 8 — I've left out the .CPP files, but you can download them plus more from *CUJ*'s FTP site). `DBXface` manages the connection and `recordset` objects required for reading or writing the database.

Class `Query` is an interface for building and executing queries and performing read-only operations on result sets. `Update` provides methods for updating or creating an object's row in the database. To integrate query and update capability with an object, objects derived from `Persist` cooperate with classes derived from `Query` and `Update`.

As Figure 6 illustrates, you use PFX by deriving one class each from `Query`, `Update`, and `Persist`. `EmpRecSet`, which Class Wizard builds for you, inherits from `CRecordset`. As you can see in Listing 9, you must provide overrides for the virtual functions `getObjID`, `getDesc`, and `SQLName`, in addition to defining member functions to access the fields.

`Query`'s criteria-selection methods call `SQLName` to get the column names that correspond to the object's attributes. The test program in Listing 10 shows that you can specify selection criteria in two different ways:

1. store the desired SQL `WHERE` clause in the filter data member of the underlying recordset, or

2. build the `WHERE` clause with the criteria-building functions from the `Query` class. The latter is more tedious but doesn't require that users know SQL or the exact names of fields in the table. You can append any number of subclauses to be ORed with the first. You then execute the query and fetch the results.

In `EmpUpdate` (see Listing 11), you specialize `Update` by overriding `Update::getID`, which returns the value in the recordset that corresponds to the object's identifier in the table, and `Update::getIDTable`, which returns the name of an auxiliary table in the database which contains the next available identifier for new records. You must provide this table. I added the table `EmployeeID` to the North Wind database with the value 10, since there were 9 records already. (NOTE: This ID-hack is single-user only. The production version of PFX uses Oracle sequence objects, which auto-increment in a way that allows multiple concurrent users.)

To finally obtain a persistent `Employee` class (Listing 12), derive it from `Persist`, override the `write` and `remove` methods (these are the most challenging of all), and provide accessors to retrieve and modify attributes as needed. The test program in Listing 13 updates an existing object and creates a new one.

Summary

The architecture presented here lends itself well to heterogeneous environments which are subject to change. The modularity of objects allows you to define systems in layers so that they are more easily maintainable and pluggable. The production implementation supports simultaneous users through the ODBC connection mechanism. Each user gets his or her own `Connection` object which acts as a handle to PFX functionality. We support transactions through the `CDatabase` methods `BeginTrans`, `CommitTrans`, and `Rollback`, which pass the corresponding SQL command on to the database. This means that transactions cannot span multiple databases. You can fix this limitation, however, by using a transaction manager, such as `Tuxedo`. PFX has low overhead, performs well, and is flexible enough to accommodate any objects you want to make persistent.

References

"Developing a Client-server Strategy," Final Report 102, Index Foundation/CSC, 1995, p. 3.

"Implementing Business Objects," Final Report 104, Index Foundation/CSC, October 1995, p. 31.

Listing 1: Header file representing Employees table

```
// EmpRecSet.h :
// Header generated by Class Wizard
//

#if !defined(EMPRECSET_H)
#define EMPRECSET_H

#include <afxdb.h>
/////////////////////////////////////////////
// EmpRecSet recordset

class EmpRecSet : public CRecordset
{
public:
    EmpRecSet(CDatabase* pDatabase = NULL);
    DECLARE_DYNAMIC(EmpRecSet)

// Field/Param Data
    //{{AFX_FIELD(EmpRecSet, CRecordset)
    long    m_Employee_ID;
    CString m_Last_Name;
    CString m_First_Name;
    CString m_Home_Phone;
    long    m_Reports_To;
    //}}AFX_FIELD


// Overrides
    // ClassWizard generated virtual
                  // function overrides
    //{{AFX_VIRTUAL(EmpRecSet)
    public:
    // Default connection string
    virtual CString GetDefaultConnect();
    // Default SQL for Recordset
    virtual CString GetDefaultSQL();
     // RFX support
    virtual void
                  DoFieldExchange(CFieldExchange* pFX);
    //}}AFX_VIRTUAL

// Implementation
#ifdef _DEBUG
    virtual void AssertValid() const;
    virtual void Dump(CDumpContext& dc) const;
#endif
};

#endif

/* End of File */
```

Listing 2: Implements EmpRecSet class

```
// EmpRecset.cpp:
// implementation generated by Class Wizard
//

#include "EmpRecSet.h"

#ifdef _DEBUG
#define new DEBUG_NEW
#undef THIS_FILE
static char THIS_FILE[] = __FILE__;
#endif

///////////////////////////////////////////
// EmpRecset

IMPLEMENT_DYNAMIC(EmpRecSet, CRecordset)

EmpRecSet::EmpRecSet(CDatabase* pdb)
        : CRecordset(pdb)
{
    //{{AFX_FIELD_INIT(EmpRecSet)
    m_Employee_ID = 0;
    m_Last_Name = _T("");
    m_First_Name = _T("");
    m_Home_Phone = _T("");
    m_Reports_To = 0;
    m_nFields = 5;
    //}}AFX_FIELD_INIT
    m_nDefaultType = snapshot;
}


CString EmpRecSet::GetDefaultConnect()
{
    return _T("ODBC;DSN=North Wind");
}

CString EmpRecSet::GetDefaultSQL()
{
    return _T("[Employees]");
}

void
EmpRecSet::DoFieldExchange(CFieldExchange* pFX)
{
//{{AFX_FIELD_MAP(EmpRecSet)
pFX->SetFieldType(CFieldExchange::outputColumn);
    RFX_Long(pFX, _T("[Employee ID]"),
                            m_Employee_ID);
    RFX_Text(pFX, _T("[Last Name]"),
                            m_Last_Name);
```

```
    RFX_Text(pFX, _T("[First Name]"),
                           m_First_Name);
    RFX_Text(pFX, _T("[Home Phone]"),
                           m_Home_Phone);
    RFX_Long(pFX, _T("[Reports To]"),
                           m_Reports_To);
    //}}AFX_FIELD_MAP
}

/////////////////////////////////////////////////
// EmpRecSet diagnostics

#ifdef _DEBUG
void EmpRecSet::AssertValid() const
{
    CRecordset::AssertValid();
}

void EmpRecSet::Dump(CDumpContext& dc) const
{
    CRecordset::Dump(dc);
}
#endif //_DEBUG

//End of File
```

Listing 3: Illustrates use of `CDatabase` and `CRecordset`

```
// Test1.cpp

#include "EmpRecSet.h"
#include <iostream.h>
#include <fstream.h>

main()
{
    // Connect to Database:
    CDatabase db;
    db.Open(0,FALSE,TRUE,
                          "ODBC;DSN=North Wind");

    // Define/populate recordset:
    EmpRecSet e(&db);
    e.m_strFilter = "[Employee ID] > 5";
    e.Open();

    // Print data:
    ofstream outf("Employee1.out",
                                ios::trunc | ios::out);
    while (!e.IsEOF())
    {
        outf << '{' << e.m_Employee_ID
             << ',' << e.m_Last_Name
```

```
            << ',' << e.m_First_Name
            << ',' << e.m_Home_Phone
            << ',' << e.m_Reports_To
                           << '}' << endl;
        e.MoveNext();
    }
    return 0;
}

/* Output:
{6,Suyama,Michael,(71) 555-7773,5}
{7,King,Jonathan,(71) 555-5598,5}
{8,Callahan,Linda,(206) 555-1189,2}
{9,Dodsworth,Annabella,(71) 555-4444,5}
*/

//End of File
```

Listing 4: Encapsulates `CDatabase` connectivity

```
// Connect.h

#if !defined(CONNECT_H)
#define CONNECT_H

#include <afx.h>      // For BOOL and CString
#include <afxdb.h>    // For CDatabase

class Connection : public CDatabase
{
public:
    static Connection* create(const CString& conSpec,BOOL readOnly = FALSE);

    long attach();    // Increments # clients
    long detach();    // Decrements # clients
                               // (self-destructs at 0)
    long nClients() const;
    void commit();
    void rollback();

private:
    long refCount;    // # clients using the
                               // connection

    // Only Connection::create can
               // instantiate Connections:
    Connection();
    ~Connection();
};

#endif

/* End of File */
```

Listing 5: Abstract interface class for DBMS access

```
// DBXFace.h:

#if !defined(DBXFACE_H)
#define DBXFACE_H

#include "Connect.h"

class DBXFace
{
public:
    virtual ~DBXFace();
    Connection* getConnection() const;

protected:
    DBXFace(CRecordset*, Connection*);
    CRecordset* rsetp;
    Connection* connectp;

private:
    // Disallowed operations
    DBXFace(const DBXFace&);
    void operator=(const DBXFace&);
};

inline Connection*
DBXFace::getConnection() const
{
    return connectp;
}

inline DBXFace::DBXFace(CRecordset* rp,
                                      Connection* cp)
{
    rsetp = rp;
    connectp = cp;
    cp->attach();
}

inline DBXFace::~DBXFace()
{
    delete rsetp;
    connectp->detach();
}

#endif

/* End of File */
```

Listing 6: Abstract class for reading a database

```
// Query.h:
#if !defined(QUERY_H)
#define QUERY_H

#include "DBXFace.h"
#include "Connect.h"

struct SortSpec
{
    int field;
    int order;
};

class Query : public DBXFace
{
public:
    BOOL execute(UINT = CRecordset::snapshot);

    // Query navigation functions
    BOOL first();
    BOOL last();
    BOOL next();
    BOOL prev();
    BOOL move(long);
    BOOL isEmpty() const;
    BOOL isEOF() const;
    BOOL isBOF() const;
    long getRecordCount() const;

    // Query-building functions
    virtual char* SQLName(int) const = 0;
    void startSelect();
    void addSelectCriteria(int,
                                     const CString&);
    void addSelect();
    void endSelect();
    void resetSelect();

    void startOrder();
    void addOrderCriteria(int, int);
    void endOrder();
    void resetOrder();

    // Accessors for attributes retrieved
    // from table
    virtual long getObjID() const = 0;
    virtual CString getDesc() const = 0;

    // Accessors for this class
    CString getFilter() const;
    CString getSort() const;
    void setFilter(const CString& filt);
```

```
    void setSort(const CString& srt);

protected:
    Query(CRecordset*, Connection*);
    CString buildClause(int, const CString&);

    CString filter;
    CString sort;

private:
    enum {MAXSORTSPEC = 10};
    SortSpec sortSpecs[MAXSORTSPEC];
    int nSortSpecs;
    BOOL newClause;

    // Disallowed ops:
    Query(const Query&);
    void operator=(const Query&);
};

#endif

/* End of File */
```

Listing 7: Abstract class for writing to a database

```
// Update.h:

#if !defined(UPDATE_H)
#define UPDATE_H

// All classes derived from class Update
              // have protected ctors, and the associated
              // business object class must be a friend,
              // e.g., class Employee is a friend to class
              // EmpUpdate (to allow an Employee object to
              // instantiate an EmpUpdate object). This
              // enforces the policy that updates can only
              // be done through objects.

#include "DBXFace.h"

class Update : public DBXFace
{
public:
    BOOL write();
    virtual long getID() const = 0;

protected:
    Update(CRecordset*, Connection*);
    long nextID();
    virtual CString getIDTable() const = 0;
```

```
private:
    // Disallowed ops:
    Update(const Update&);
    void operator=(const Update&);
};

#endif

/* End of File */
```

Listing 8: Holds object identifier

```
// Persist.h

#if !defined(PERSIST_H)
#define PERSIST_H

#include <afx.h>        // For BOOL
#include "Connect.h"

class Persist
{
public:
    virtual ~Persist();
    virtual BOOL write() = 0;
    virtual BOOL remove() = 0;
    operator void*() const;

    // Accessors
    long getObjID() const;
    Connection* getConnection() const;

protected:
    Persist(Connection* cp, long id = 0L);

    // Attributes common to all persistent
                // objects:
    long objID;
    Connection* connectp;
    BOOL valid;

private:
    // Disallowed operations
    Persist(const Persist&);
    void operator=(const Persist&);
};

inline Persist::Persist(Connection* cp,
                                    long id)
{
    objID = id;
    connectp = cp;
    connectp->attach();
```

```
    // Must be determined in concrete class
    valid = FALSE;
}

inline long Persist::getObjID() const
{
    return objID;
}

inline Connection*
              Persist::getConnection() const
{
    return connectp;
}

inline Persist::~Persist()
{
    connectp->detach();
}

inline Persist::operator void*() const
{
    return valid ? (void*) this : 0;
}

#endif

/* End of File */
```

Listing 9: Inheriting from class `Query`

```
// EmpQuery.h

#if !defined(EMP_QUERY_H)
#define EMP_QUERY_H

#include <afx.h>    // For CString
#include <afxdb.h>  // For CRecordset
                                  // constants
#include "query.h"

class EmpQuery : public Query
{
    friend class EmpUpdate;
    friend class Employee;

public:
    EmpQuery(Connection*);

    // Overrides:
    virtual long getObjID() const;
    virtual CString getDesc() const;
    virtual char* SQLName(int) const;
```

```
    // Accessors:
    CString getLastName() const;
    CString getFirstName() const;
    CString getHomePhone() const;
    long getReportsTo() const;

    enum {TABLE_NAME, OBJ_ID, LAST_NAME,
                        FIRST_NAME, HOME_PHONE,
                        REPORTS_TO};

protected:
    enum {NFIELDS = 5};
    static char* queryTable[NFIELDS+1];
};

#endif
/* End of File */
```

Listing 10: Uses a customized Query object

```
// Test2.cpp:

#include "Connect.h"
#include "EmpQuery.h"
#include <iostream.h>

void displayResults(EmpQuery&);

main()
{
    // Connect to Database:
    Connection *cp =
                  Connection::create("ODBC"
                                    "DSN=North Wind",
                                    TRUE);

    // Define Query with criteria via
              // Filter String:
    EmpQuery q(cp);
    q.setFilter("[Employee ID] > 5");
    q.execute();
    displayResults(q);
    cout << endl;

    // Define Query with Query functions:
    q.startSelect();
    q.addSelectCriteria(EmpQuery::OBJ_ID,
                                  "field > 5");
    q.endSelect();
    q.execute();
    displayResults(q);
```

```
    cp->detach();
    return 0;
}

void displayResults(EmpQuery& q)
{
    while (!q.isEOF())
    {
        cout << '{' << q.getObjID()
             << ',' << q.getLastName()
             << ',' << q.getFirstName()
             << ',' << q.getHomePhone()
             << ',' << q.getReportsTo()
                          << '}' << endl;
        q.next();
    }
}

/* Output:
{6,Suyama,Michael,(71) 555-7773,5}
{7,King,Jonathan,(71) 555-5598,5}
{8,Callahan,Linda,(206) 555-1189,2}
{9,Dodsworth,Annabella,(71) 555-4444,5}

{6,Suyama,Michael,123-456-7890,5}
{7,King,Jonathan,(71) 555-5598,5}
{8,Callahan,Linda,(206) 555-1189,2}
{9,Dodsworth,Annabella,(71) 555-4444,5}
*/
//End of File
```

Listing 11: Inherits from Update

```
// EmpUpdate.h

#if !defined(EMP_UPDATE_H)
#define EMP_UPDATE_H

#include "Update.h"
#include "EmpQuery.h"

class Employee;
class Connection;

class EmpUpdate : public Update
{
    friend class Employee;

public:
    void edit(const Employee&);
    long getID() const;

protected:
```

```
    EmpUpdate(Connection*, long id);
    CString getIDTable() const;
};

inline CString EmpUpdate::getIDTable() const
{
    // Table with next available Object ID
    return "[Employee ID]";
}

#endif
/* End of File */
```

Listing 12: A persistent class

```
// Employee.h

#if !defined(EMPLOYEE_H)
#define EMPLOYEE_H

#include <afx.h>
#include "Persist.h"

class EmpQuery;
class Connection;

class Employee : public Persist
{
public:
    Employee(Connection* cp, long id = 0L);
    Employee(const EmpQuery&);

    // Accessors:
    CString getLastName() const;
    CString getFirstName() const;
    CString getHomePhone() const;
    long getReportsTo() const;
    void setLastName(const CString&);
    void setFirstName(const CString&);
    void setHomePhone(const CString&);
    void setReportsTo(long);

    // Business Functions:
    Employee* getSuperior() const;

    // Persistence overides:
    virtual BOOL write();
    virtual BOOL remove();

private:
    CString lastName;
    CString firstName;
    CString homePhone;
```

```
    long reportsTo;

    // Disabled operations
                 // (i.e., not implemented)
    Employee(const Employee&);
    void operator=(const Employee&);
};

#endif

/* End of File */
```

Listing 13: Tests the Employee business class

```
// Test3.cpp:

#include "Connect.h"
#include "Employee.h"
#include <iostream.h>

void displayEmployee(const Employee&);

main()
{
    // Connect to Database:
    Connection *cp =
                      Connection::create("ODBC"
                                         "DSN=North Wind");

    // Retrieve an employee & boss:
    Employee emp(cp,6);
    displayEmployee(emp);
    Employee* boss = emp.getSuperior();
    cout << "Reports To: ";
    displayEmployee(*boss);
    delete boss;          // Dynamic object!

    // Update the object on disk:
    emp.setHomePhone("123-456-7890");
    emp.write();

    // Verify the change:
    Employee emp2(cp,6);
    displayEmployee(emp2);

    // Create new employee:
    Employee emp3(cp);
    emp3.setLastName("Claus");
    emp3.setFirstName("Santa");
    emp3.setHomePhone("unlisted");
    emp3.setReportsTo(1);
    emp3.write();
```

```
    // Verify the change:
    Employee emp4(cp,6);
    displayEmployee(emp4);

    cp->detach();
    return 0;
}

void displayEmployee(const Employee& e)
{
    cout << '{' << e.getObjID()
         << ',' << e.getLastName()
         << ',' << e.getFirstName()
         << ',' << e.getHomePhone()
                       << '}' << endl;
}

/* Output:
{6,Suyama,Michael,(71) 555-7773}
Reports To: {5,Buchanan,B. L.,(71) 555-4848}
{6,Suyama,Michael,123-456-7890}
{10,Claus,Santa,unlisted}
*/
//End of File
```

A Database Cache Manager from MFC Components

Pete Rail

The Microsoft Foundation Class (MFC) Library provides easy-to-use collection classes. You can use these predefined classes "as is" to manage your application lists, or you can extend them though inheritance and combination (see Figure 1 for an overview of the stock MFC collection classes). The benefit of using these prewritten classes is clear — reduced development and debugging time. You can concentrate on what is unique about your program while saving yourself the "grunt work" of building and debugging custom components from scratch. And because the MFC classes are so basic, they make an excellent starting point for your own type-safe classes.

There is more to extending MFC collection classes than just hiding them in type-safe wrappers, however. By adroitly combining existing MFC raw materials,

Pete Rail is a Senior Systems Engineer with Electronic Data Systems Corporation in Plano, Texas. He can be reached on CompuServe at 71233,2575. *Reprinted courtesy of* Windows Developer Journal.

you can build new, powerful collection classes that exploit the synergy among the available MFC building blocks. In this article, I present a simple, high-speed cache manager assembled from available MFC components. The Simple Cache Manager not only demonstrates a technique for extending MFC classes, it also provides a reusable class that you can easily plug into your MFC-based applications.

Cashing In on Caches

Despite the hype about grand improvements in disk and network speed, application response time never seems fast enough. One technique for improving application speed is to save previously accessed data in memory for quick retrieval. This constitutes a data cache. Data caching is a commonly employed method of avoiding unnecessary disk or network I/O, albeit at the cost of some local memory. Ram disks are a well-known example of a data cache. The family of functions that access and manipulate Windows `.ini` files is a lesser known case of data caching. The implicit assumption of a data cache is that if you accessed something before, you'll likely access that same thing again.

Judicious use of data caches in client/server applications can make the difference between a sluggish, resource-hungry headache and a satisfying high-performance solution. One commonly cited performance problem can help illuminate this discussion: the database bottleneck. A natural bottleneck forms when many client applications submit requests to a single database server. Although database servers (for example, Sybase) respond admirably to this challenge by maintaining a cache of recently requested data in the server, they may still bog down under the load of many query-hungry clients.

One way to take some of the load off the centralized server is to cache query results on the client machine. Since client-side caches adapt to the application user's behavior by maintaining a list of recently used data, results can be returned more quickly than would be possible for even the fastest cen-

Collection Type	Inserts	Lookups	Allows Duplicates?	Internal Representation
List	Fast	Slow	Yes	Doubly-linked list of objects
Array	Slow	Slow	Yes	Dynamically sized, integer indexed array of objects
Map	Fast	Fast	No*	Hash table that associates a key with a value object

*Refer to MFC Class Library User's Guide for exceptions to this rule.

Figure 1: ***MFC collection classes.***

Function	Description
Lookup	Returns the CCacheObject pointer associated with a key value.
SetAt	Inserts a CCacheObject into the cache, replacing any existing object with the same key.
RemoveKey	Removes a CCacheObject from the cache.
RemoveAll	Removes all the objects from the cache.
GetStartPosition	Returns the position of the first object in the cache.
GetNextAssoc	Gets the next object in the cache (usefule for interating through the cache entries).
GetCount	Returns the maximum number of entries allowed in the cache.
IsEmpty	Tests if the cache contains any CCacheObjects.
IsFull	Tests if the cache has reached its capacity.
GetEntryLimit	Returns the maximum number of entries in the cache.
SetEntryLimit	Adjusts the maximum number of entreis in the cache.
GetName	Returns the name assigned to this cache.
SetName	Sets the name of this cache.
GetStats	Returns cache access statistics (i.e., hits, misses, insets, removes).

Figure 2: *CCache services.*

tral server. If the cache is effective, it will reduce the number of requests sent to the server and improve the average response time for all clients. Under best-case conditions, the application can almost appear to anticipate the user's requests. This can make even the most curmudgeonly user thankful, at least for a moment.

Although client-side data caching appears to be the ideal cure for client/server performance ills, a note of caution is in order. If the objects you plan to cache can be updated, then you must design a checkout strategy to prevent overlapping updates, and this may be complicated. In fact, this consideration may rule out a client-side cache for some applications; however, the client-side cache strategy is still viable for the many applications that present historical information and other static data, like bitmapped images. A more simple and obvious approach to protecting data integrity is to cache only non-volatile data: this is the method used by the Simple Cache Manager.

Inside the Simple Cache Manager

I developed the Simple Cache Manager to meet the following requirements:

- Exhibit good performance (fast lookups)
- Employ a least-recently-used (LRU) strategy
- Track cache access statistics (hits, misses, inserts, removes)
- Be flexible enough for reuse in a variety of applications
- Be simple to code and understand

A hash table and a least-recently-used (LRU) list form the core of the Simple Cache Manager. The hash table allows quick lookups of cached entries by key, and the LRU list is used to monitor the age and number of cached items. The use of the LRU strategy is basic to cache design: when the cache is full and an entry must be added, the least-recently-used entry in the cache is removed to make room for a new one. In addition, when an entry is looked up, it is promoted to the head of the LRU list to reflect its most-recently-used status. The effect of the LRU strategy is that commonly accessed objects are retained in the cache for quick retrieval.

A careful inventory of the strengths and weaknesses of the available MFC containers made clear which combination would perform well as a cache manager. Because the MFC map classes provide an adequate hash table implementation, and the `CObList` class contained all the functions required for an LRU, building the Simple Cache Manager (`CCache`) class was a snap. I just added some supporting code to integrate the MFC classes and to track cache access statistics. The result is in `ccache.h` (Listing 1) and `ccache.cpp` (Listing 2).

I chose the `CMapStringToOb` class for the hash table component of the cache manager because text is a common, simple key representation. It also makes a good illustration. If strings are not a good match for the key definition in your problem, consider extending `CCache` to use one of the other map collections, such as `CMapPtrToPtr` or `CMapWordToOb`.

Using the CCache class

Incorporating caching into your MFC-based application is simple and painless. You must derive the objects that you plan to cache from the `CCacheObject` class and write two member functions, `Duplicate()` and `GetKey()`. `CCache` only manages objects from the `CCacheObject` class, so by deriving your class from `CCacheObject`, you ensure compatibility. The `Duplicate()` member function is responsible for making an exact copy of the object. Write your `Duplicate()` function so that a "deep copy" is performed because `CCache` requires a complete copy of the object, not just a pointer to it.

The `GetKey()` member function is expected to return your object's unique key as a `CString`.

To avoid memory leaks, be sure to declare a virtual destructor for your derived class. Because `CCache` can cache any object that can both duplicate and identify itself with a unique key, there are few objects that it cannot manage. After you have defined the `CCacheObject` support functions for your class, you are free to store instances of your class inside a `CCache`.

The available `CCache` services are briefly described in Figure 2. Those of you who have used the `CMapStringToOb` class will notice that I have mimicked its operator names as well as adding a few my own.

A Simple Example

The sample code fragment in Figure 3 demonstrates the `CCache` interface. The code is intended to show how a `CCache` collection might be used to improve the response time of keyed reads on a networked personnel database. First, the code creates a `CCache` instance called `Photos`. The cache can hold a maximum

```
CPhoto* pPhoto;
CString zEmpNumber;
int nHits, nMisses, nInserts, nRemoves;
// ...

CCache* pCache = new CCache( "Photos", 10 );
// ...

while( PromptEmpNumber( zEmpNumber ) != NULL )
{
    if( pPhoto = pCache->Lookup( zEmpNumber )) != NULL )
    {
        // Photo found in cache, server access bypassed
    }
    else
    {
        // Photo not found in cache, access server
        pPhoto = GetPhoto( zEmpNumber );

        // Add Photo to cache
        pCache->SetAt( (const char*) zEmpNumber, pPhoto );
    }
}
// ...

// Display statistics about cache activity
pCache->GetStats( nHits, nMisses, nInserts, nRemoves );
cout <<<< "Cache Statistics follow" <<<< endl;
cout <<<< "Hits=" <<<< nHits <<<< " Misses=" <<<< nMisses <<<< endl;
cout <<<< "Inserts=" <<<< nInserts <<<< " Removes=" <<<< nRemoves <<<< endl;
/* End of File */
```

Figure 3: ***Demonstrating the CCache class.***

of ten digitized employee photographs held in `CPhoto` objects. Static graphics of this kind are ideal candidates for caching, since they may be large, and thus slow to retrieve.

After creating the cache object, the code prompts the user for the employee number of the subject to display. The code calls `CCache::Lookup()` to probe the cache for a match, and if none is found, calls `GetPhoto()` to search the database. Since this call involves a network request to a server, it is a relatively slow, expensive operation. To avoid an expensive re-query of the same employee, the photograph is cached locally. When the user requests this employee again, the request can be satisfied in the time it takes to probe the cache. No network or database waits are incurred because no request is sent to a server. If the user does not request the same employee again, the photograph stored in the cache will be freed when the cache exceeds ten entries.

When the user finishes looking at employee photographs, the code displays cache statistics showing the number of cache hits, misses, inserts, and replaces. These statistics can help the developer (or user) tune the application by adjusting the number of cache entries. As a rule, you should try to strike a balance between access speed and memory use. If your cache contains too few entries, then your application may perform slowly; if your cache contains too many entries, you waste memory. You'll need to experiment to find the optimum balance for your application.

Conclusion

MFC collection classes may be handy right out of the box, but they can also be combined to form new, flexible components. The cache manager described here was built chiefly from available MFC components: it is small, flexible and easy to integrate with your MFC-based applications. You may be surprised by how little code it took to implement this reusable class.

Although I've presented the Simple Cache Manager in a multi-user, client/server context, you could use it on single-user systems if you are willing to trade memory for speed.

The Simple Cache Manager is not for everyone, however. Although it could play a supporting role in the development of a more complicated approach, it is intended to manage non-volatile objects in a multi-user environment. This is still an important niche, given the number of systems that deal with imaging, billing, or other historical data. The myriad decision support systems that track day-old data can also benefit from the performance gains that a client-side cache can offer.

Listing 1: ccache.h—Interface to CCache class

```
// File:   ccache.h
// Author: Pete Rail November 1994
// Copyright (c) EDS, 1994.
// Readers of Windows/DOS Developer's Journal are hereby
// granted a nonexclusive, royalty-free license to use, modify
// and distribute this program.

#ifndef CCACHE_H
#define CCACHE_H

// all objects placed in cache must be derived from CCacheObject
class CCacheObject : public CObject
{
public:
    virtual CCacheObject* Duplicate(void) = 0;
    virtual const char* GetKey( CString& keyValue ) const = 0;
};

class CCache : public CMapStringToOb
{
public:
    CCache( const char* name, int numEntries=1 );
    ~CCache();
    BOOL IsFull() const;
    CCacheObject* Lookup( const char* key );
    void RemoveAll();
    BOOL RemoveKey( const char* key );
    void SetAt( const char* key, CCacheObject* newValue );

// Get/Set for private variables
    void SetEntryLimit( int numEntries );
    int GetEntryLimit() const { return m_EntryLimit; }
    void SetName( const char* name ) { m_Name = name; }
    const char* GetName() const { return (const char*)m_Name; }
    void GetStats( int& hits, int& misses, int& inserts, int& removes )
const;

private:
    void InitStats();

protected:
    CObList m_LRU;          // least-recently used list

private:
    CString m_Name;         // caller supplied name of cache
    int m_EntryLimit;       // max entries allowed in cache
    int m_Hits;             // # successful...
    int m_Misses;           // ...and unsuccessful searches
    int m_Inserts;          // # adds to cache
    int m_Removes;          // # explict/implict removes
};

#endif
/* End of File */
```

Listing 2: ccache.cpp—Implementation of CCache class

```
// File:   ccache.cpp
// Author: Pete Rail November 1994
// Copyright (c) EDS, 1994.
// Readers of Windows/DOS Developer's Journal are hereby
// granted a nonexclusive, royalty-free license to use, modify
// and distribute this program.

#include "stdafx.h"
#include "ccache.h"

CCache :: CCache( const char* name, int numEntries /* =1 */ )
{
    m_Name       = name;
    m_EntryLimit = __max( numEntries, 1 );  // allow no less than 1 entry
in cache
    InitStats();
}

CCache :: ~CCache()
{
    RemoveAll();
}

void CCache :: GetStats( int& hits, int& misses, int& inserts, int& removes
) const
{
    hits = m_Hits; misses = m_Misses; inserts = m_Inserts, removes =
m_Removes;
}

void CCache :: InitStats()
{
    m_Hits      = 0;
    m_Misses    = 0;
    m_Inserts   = 0;
    m_Removes   = 0;
}

BOOL CCache :: IsFull() const
{
    return m_LRU.GetCount() >= m_EntryLimit;
}

CCacheObject* CCache :: Lookup( const char* key )
{
    BOOL b;
    CCacheObject* rValue;

    if( (b = CMapStringToOb::Lookup( key, (CObject*&)rValue )) == TRUE )
    {   // make this object most-recently used, promote to head of m_LRU
        POSITION pos = m_LRU.Find( rValue );   // linear search
        ASSERT( pos );
```

```
        m_LRU.RemoveAt( pos );
        m_LRU.AddHead( rValue );

        // make a new object and copy object from cache to new object
        // this is the address of the one to return.
        rValue = rValue->Duplicate();
        m_Hits++;
    }
    else
    {
        m_Misses++;
    }

    return (b == TRUE) ? rValue : NULL;
}


void CCache :: RemoveAll()
{
    POSITION pos;

    for( pos = m_LRU.GetHeadPosition(); pos != NULL; )
    {   // release memory for all objects in cache
        delete m_LRU.GetNext( pos );
    }

    CMapStringToOb::RemoveAll(); // release memory for map
    m_LRU.RemoveAll();           // ... and list
    InitStats();                 // clear statistics
}

BOOL CCache :: RemoveKey( const char* key )
{
    CCacheObject* rValue;

    if( (rValue = Lookup( key )) != NULL )
    {
        CMapStringToOb::RemoveKey( key );   // remove obj from map
        delete m_LRU.RemoveHead();          // & cleanup LRU too
        m_Removes++;
    }

    return rValue != NULL;
}

void CCache :: SetAt( const char* key, CCacheObject* newValue )
{
    CString oldKey;
    CCacheObject* myObj;

    if( CMapStringToOb::Lookup( key, (CObject*&)myObj ) )

        RemoveKey( key );  // try to remove in case it's a duplicate
```

```
    if( IsFull() )
    {
        CCacheObject* old = (CCacheObject*) m_LRU.RemoveTail();
        ASSERT(old);
        // clean up map and release cached object
        CMapStringToOb::RemoveKey( old->GetKey( oldKey ) );
        delete old;
        m_Removes++;
    }

    // make a copy for the cache and make it most-recently-used
    CMapStringToOb::SetAt( key, myObj = newValue->Duplicate() );
    m_LRU.AddHead( myObj );
    m_Inserts++;
}

// shrink the cache if necessary (min size = 1 entry)
void CCache :: SetEntryLimit( int numEntries )
{
    CString oldKey;
    m_EntryLimit = __max( numEntries, 1 );

    while( m_EntryLimit < m_LRU.GetCount() )
    {
        CCacheObject* old = (CCacheObject*) m_LRU.RemoveTail();
        ASSERT(old);

        CMapStringToOb::RemoveKey( old->GetKey( oldKey ) );
        delete old;
        m_Removes++;
    }
}
//End of File
```

Accessing Binary Database Fields With MFC

Greg Johnson

It is no longer uncommon for databases to contain binary data in some form. For example, a database for a real estate firm might store a bitmap containing a digitized picture of each house along with other data pertaining to the house, such as address, price, and so on. This article shows how to use MFC's database classes on an interface for storing and retrieving binary image data.

The newer databases support Binary Large OBject (BLOB) data columns (or most of them do in some form). Databases supported by VC++ are either

---

Greg Johnson is a Contract Consultant currently on assignment to Fidelity Investments, Inc. in Boston, MA. He has been programming in Windows since 1989, and in C++ since 1990. He has used MFC for the last 3 years for applications including document/ image database storage and retrieval, manufacturing process control, automated pharmaceuticals/drug testing, and digital video on demand systems. Reprinted courtesy of Windows Developer Journal.

multiple-file databases, where multiple files make up the database, or single-file databases, where the entire database is contained in a single file. I have chosen the MS-Access ISAM (Indexed Sequential Access Method) single-file database as the basis for this article and the accompanying demonstration program. Walking through this example will help you to understand what you have to do to create and use databases that contain binary data with MFC.

The entire program is not listed here, but it is set up in the usual way with the VC++ App Wizard, Class Wizard, and App Studio tools. The focus here is on two classes shown in listings 1 through 4: the `dbBmpRecordset` class, which is derived from the MFC `CRecordset` class, and the `dbBitmap` class, which is derived from the MFC `CBitmap` class. These two classes provide the interface to the database table named `BITMAPS` in the `bmp.mdb` database file.

Setting Up the Database

The first step is to use MS-Query to create the database. Then, after you've created the database, you define a new table. In the example I'm using, the first column, "ID", is a 16-bit integer column (a "SHORT" in MS-Query); column two, "Descr", is a "TEXT" column having a maximum length of 255 characters; and column three, "Bmp", is defined as a "LONG BINARY" column (in MS-Access this shows up as an Ole Object column).

Once the database is created, you must register it with the ODBC Administrator, which VC++ installs in the Control Panel. At this point you are ready to write code to access the database.

Storing Bitmaps

The first step here is to use Class Wizard to derive a class from `Crecordset`; in the example, I called it `dbBmpRecordset`. The Class Wizard will ask for the database source (which you defined in the ODBC Administrator), and then the table name; in this case "Bitmaps" is the name of the table. The result will be a class declaration header file similar to that in `dbbmprec.h` (Listing 1). You see that the member variables are an `int m_ID`, a `CString` named `m_Descr`, and a `CLongBinary` named `m_Bmp`. This `CLongBinary` class is where binary data is stored, but it requires special treatment. The contents of the `CLongBinary` class are a `HANDLE` to global memory and the size of the data within that global handle. `dbbmprec.cpp` (Listing 2) contains the implementation of `dbBmpRecordset`. These two files are pretty much just what Class Wizard created, but with two member "accessor" methods

```
int& qryID(void);
CString& qryDescr(void);
```

to provide access to the "ID" and "Description" fields in the database table, and simply return a reference to the appropriate variable.

The two methods added for placing a bitmap into the `CLongBinary` field and retrieving a bitmap from the `CLongBinary` field are:

```
BOOL setBitmap(dbBitmap* bmp);
BOOL qryBitmap(dbBitmap* bmp);
```

Both of these methods take a pointer to a `dbBitmap` class (which is derived from `CBitmap` and explained in detail further on). First, I'll explain the `setBitmap()` method step by step, since it's impossible to retrieve a bitmap from the database until one is available.

`setBitMap()` starts by calling `CRecordset::IsOpen()`, just to verify that the recordset is valid. Next, the function makes sure that both the pointer to the bitmap and the `HANDLE` to the bitmap are non-`NULL`. These checks simply confirm that I have a valid `CBitmap` instance. `setBitMap()` then extracts information about the bitmap from the underlying `CGdiObject` class into a `BITMAP` structure with the call:

```
pBitmap->GetObject(sizeof(BITMAP),&bm);
```

This places the bitmap's information into a `BITMAP` structure that is used to determine the size of the bitmap. From the `BITMAP` structure, I calculate the number of bytes needed to hold all the bits in this bitmap. The result of this calculation, plus the size of the `BITMAP struct`, will be used to allocate the memory in the `CLongBinary` object.

```
sz= ((bm.bmWidthBytes * bm.bmHeight) * bm.bmPlanes);
```

Next, I allocate a zero-filled buffer to hold the bitmap:

```
bufr= new BYTE[sz + sizeof(BITMAP) + 1];
memset(bufr,'\0',sz + sizeof(BITMAP) + 1);
```

The actual bitmap bits will get stored right after the `BITMAP` information structure, so I create a temporary pointer to that location:

```
tmp= bufr + sizeof(BITMAP);
```

Then I copy the `BITMAP` structure into the beginning of the buffer:

```
memcpy(bufr,&bm,sizeof(BITMAP));
```

Next, I retrieve the bitmap's graphic bits from the `CBitmap` object, copying them into the buffer after the `BITMAP` structure:

```
pBitmap->GetBitmapBits(sz,tmp);
```

Now the bufr variable is pointing to a BITMAP structure that is followed by the bitmap's data bits.

Once the bitmap information and bits reside in a contiguous block of memory, they can be stored in the CLongBinary object. If the CLongBinary already has a valid HANDLE, I free it. Then I allocate a global memory handle, lock it, copy the bitmap in the memory buffer into the new global memory, and unlock it.

```
if(m_Bmp.m_hData)
    GlobalFree(m_Bmp.m_hData);
m_Bmp.m_hData= GlobalAlloc(GHND,
    sz+sizeof(BITMAP)+1);
tmp= (BYTE*)GlobalLock(m_Bmp.m_hData);
memcpy(tmp,bufr,sz + sizeof(BITMAP));
GlobalUnlock(m_Bmp.m_hData);
```

I also have to tell the CLongBinary field how large the binary data object is. This size is used by the ODBC driver to transmit the right number of bytes to the database.

```
m_Bmp.m_dwDataLength= sz + sizeof(BITMAP);
```

The last part is the most important: you must manually call the recordset's SetFieldDirty() and SetFieldNull() methods to tell the recordset that it must save the CLongBinary field to the database. If you fail to do this, the CLongBinary field will be skipped in the Update() operation. Finally, I free up the memory I allocated:

```
SetFieldDirty(&(m_Bmp));
SetFieldNull(&(m_Bmp),FALSE);
if(bufr)
    delete[] bufr;
```

The steps above store a bitmap in the CLongBinary member variable m_Bmp, so the bitmap is ready to be written to the database table when CRecordset::Update() gets called. In this example, Update() will be called by the dbBitmap class later.

Retrieving a Bitmap

When you read a record containing a bitmap, the bitmap will reside in a CLongBinary object, which is not a convenient format for display. The qryBitmap() method copies the CLongBinary object into the dbBitmap object you supply it. This is not quite the reverse of the setBitmap() method, but is much easier. First, if the dbBitmap object's internal HANDLE is not NULL, it presumably contains an HBITMAP that must be destroyed. Then, if there is a current record, the CLongBinary object's global HANDLE is locked to provide a pointer to an array of bytes. Creating a bitmap for display requires a device context compatible with the current display:

```
dc.CreateDC("DISPLAY",NULL,NULL,NULL);
```

I also need a pointer from which to copy the bitmap's data bits:

```
bufr= (BYTE*)GlobalLock(m_Bmp.m_hData);
tmp= bufr + sizeof(BITMAP);
```

Next, I copy the BITMAP structure from the raw bitmap buffer into a BITMAP variable, and calculate the size of the bitmap:

```
memcpy(&bm,bufr,sizeof(BITMAP));
sz= ((bm.bmWidthBytes
    * bm.bmHeight) * bm.bmPlanes);
```

Then, using the display device context, I have the dbBitmap object create a bitmap based on the width and height of the bitmap that was stored in the database:

```
pBitmap->CreateCompatibleBitmap
    (&dc,bm.bmWidth,bm.bmHeight);
```

Last, I copy the bitmap's data bits into the newly created dbBitmap, unlock the global HANDLE, and am ready to display the bitmap.

```
pBitmap->SetBitmapBits(sz,tmp);
GlobalUnlock(m_Bmp.m_hData);
```

Database I/O

The two methods just described demonstrate how to store and retrieve a bitmap image to and from the recordset's binary data field. These do not, however, store and retrieve the fields to and from the database. The dbBitmap class, which is derived from Cbitmap, actually does the database I/O. dbBitmap is defined in db_bmp.h (Listing 3) and implemented in db_bmp.cpp (Listing 4).

Given an "ID" (column one in the "Bitmaps" table), dbBitmap can retrieve a bitmap with that key, or store a bitmap with that key. If a bitmap already exists with the specified key identifier, that record is updated to reflect any changes to that key identifier. All of this is accomplished through the two methods:

```
int store(CDatabase* db);
int fetch(int id,CDatabase* db);
```

The store() method, referencing the CDatabase object passed in, uses the dbBmpRecordset to store a bitmap to the database; the fetch() method, also referencing the CDatabase object, uses the integer identifier key to find and retrieve a bitmap. Two other variables in the dbBitmap class hold the bitmap description field and the ID field, along with "accessor" methods for each. Both the store() and fetch() methods use the TRY-CATCH exception handling mechanism to gracefully recover from database errors. Both will print an error message to the debug device (DBWin or current debug output device) if an exception is thrown.

The store() method first creates an SQL "WHERE" clause, using the CRecordset::m_strFilter to open the recordset and find any record with the current ID. The first record is made current if one exists.

```
CString filter("ID= %d");
dbBmpRecordset rs(pDB);
sprintf(rs.m_strFilter.
            GetBufferSetLength(255),
filter.GetBuffer(filter.GetLength()),
            iBmpID);
rs.m_strFilter.ReleaseBuffer(-1);
rs.Open();
rs.MoveFirst();
```

If there is a current record, the code will be editing that record. If no current record exists, then the code will be adding a new record. CRecordset::IsBOF() ("is before beginning") and CRecordset::IsEOF() ("is past end-of-file") indicate that no records were found with the same ID value as iBmpID. I also keep a flag to indicate whether or not the ID field is needed: for editing, it is not, but for adding a new record, it is.

```
if(!rs.IsBOF() && !rs.IsEOF())
    {
    rs.Edit();
    upd= TRUE;
    }
else
    rs.AddNew();
```

Next I move the data to be stored from the dbBitmap's variables to the recordset's bound variables. Note that using a recordset as a storage object may cause problems, since every time you open or close the recordset, or move through the records using MoveNext(), the contents of the recordset change. This is the purpose of dbBitmap: it holds the values as they are used by the application.

```
if(!upd)
    rs.qryID()= iBmpID;
rs.qryDescr()= szDescr;
rs.setBitmap(this);
```

Finally, I send the record to be stored in the database file, close the recordset, and return no errors.

```
rs.Update();
rs.Close();
```

The `CATCH` mechanism will be called if any of the calls to the `CRecordset` "throw" an exception. The `CATCH` in both the `store()` and `fetch()` methods is the same. Only exceptions thrown with the type `CDBException` will be caught here. The `CDBException` class will contain error information specific to the underlying ODBC driver in use. In both cases here, the `nRetCode` from the `CDBException` is returned if an error has occurred.

`dbBitmap::fetch()` retrieves the specified bitmap by its key field. An SQL "Where" clause is constructed such that if identifier 1001 is passed to the `fetch()` method, the filter string member variable would contain "ID= 1001". This is the same for both `store()` and `fetch()`. The filter is built before a recordset is opened, so that the filter is executed by the query when the recordset is opened. Then the first record is made current.

```
sprintf(rs.m_strFilter.
    GetBufferSetLength(255),
    filter.GetBuffer(filter.GetLength()),
    id);
rs.m_strFilter.ReleaseBuffer(-1);
ret= rs.Open();
rs.MoveFirst();
```

Using both `IsBOF()` and `IsEOF()`, I check to see if there is a current record; if there is, the bitmap and the description fields are copied from the recordset into the `dbBitmap` object. If there is not a current record, I return *-1* to indicate not found. I then close the recordset.

```
if(!rs.IsBOF() && !rs.IsEOF())
    {
    szDescr= rs.qryDescr();
    rs.qryBitmap(this);
    }
else
    ret= -1;
rs.Close();
```

That's all there is to it. The dbBitmap class knows how to fetch bitmaps from the database, and either edit existing bitmaps or add new bitmaps using the dbBmpRecordset class to interface to the database. This implementation makes the bitmaps in the database device-dependent; you can overcome this by adding the BITMAPINFOHEADER into the binary field.

Summary

The demonstration program on the code disk uses two dialogs to demonstrate dbBitmap and dbBmpRecordset. The first dialog has the user type the bitmap's ID and description, loads a bitmap from a .bmp file, then saves that bitmap into the database. The second dialog presents the user with a list of the bitmaps contained in the database, and when one is selected, displays that bitmap.

I created the CDatabase object and stored it in the application's CDocument class. The CDatabase object is created and opened when the CDocument class is created. This is primarily due to the longer time required to open the database connection. The CDatabase object remains open while the application is running. When the CDocument class is destroyed, so is the CDatabase object. By containing the CDatabase object in the document class, I make it available throughout the application.

Databases have become a part of the application as well as the application's target. By using databases as part of your application, you can give users the ability to make minor configuration choices, such as changing a bitmap in a toolbar. For developers, databases can provide a more uniform and less development-intensive place to hold information that once had to be tucked away in files, or in custom data resources. Given the ability of databases to hold large binary fields, such as images or other custom data structures, and the availability of those databases developers can spend more effort on increasing application functionality, rather than supporting that functionality.

Listing 1: dbbmprec.h—Definition of recordset containing bitmaps

```
#ifndef _DbBmpRec_
#define _DbBmpRec_

class dbBitmap;

//////////////////////////////////////////////////////////////////////////
// dbBmpRecordset recordset

class dbBmpRecordset : public CRecordset
    {
public:
    dbBmpRecordset(CDatabase* pDatabase);
    virtual ~dbBmpRecordset(void);
    BOOL qryBitmap(dbBitmap*);  // retrieve from binary field
```

```
    BOOL setBitmap(dbBitmap*);  // store into binary field
    int& qryID(void) // returns bitmap Identifier (key field)
        { return(m_ID); }
    CString& qryDescr(void)     // return description field
        { return(m_Descr); }

// Implementation
protected:
    // Field/Param Data
    //{{AFX_FIELD(dbBmpRecordset, CRecordset)
    int     m_ID;
    CString m_Descr;
    CLongBinary m_Bmp;
    //}}AFX_FIELD

    virtual CString GetDefaultConnect();
    virtual CString GetDefaultSQL();
    virtual void DoFieldExchange(CFieldExchange* pFX);
    DECLARE_DYNAMIC(dbBmpRecordset)
};


#endif  // _DbBmpRec_
/* End of File */
```

Listing 2: dbbmprec.cpp—Implementation of recordset containing bitmaps

```
#include "stdafx.h"
#include "db_bmp.h"

#ifndef _DbBitmap_
#   include "dbbitmap.h"
#endif
#ifndef _DbBmpRec_
#   include "dbbmprec.h"
#endif

#ifdef _DEBUG
#undef THIS_FILE
static char BASED_CODE THIS_FILE[] = __FILE__;
#define new DEBUG_NEW
#endif

/////////////////////////////////////////////////////////////
// dbBmpRecordset

IMPLEMENT_DYNAMIC(dbBmpRecordset, CRecordset)

dbBmpRecordset::dbBmpRecordset(CDatabase* pdb)
    : CRecordset(pdb)
{
    //{{AFX_FIELD_INIT(dbBmpRecordset)
```

```
    m_ID = 0;
    m_Descr = "";
    m_nFields = 3;
    //}}AFX_FIELD_INIT
}

dbBmpRecordset::~dbBmpRecordset(void)
{   }

BOOL dbBmpRecordset::qryBitmap(dbBitmap* pBitmap)
{
    BOOL ret= FALSE;
    BYTE* bufr= NULL;
    BYTE* tmp= NULL;
    BITMAP bm;
    CDC dc;
    int sz= 0;

    if(pBitmap)
        {
        if(pBitmap->m_hObject)
            ::DeleteObject(pBitmap->Detach());

        if(!IsBOF() && !IsEOF())
            {
            dc.CreateDC("DISPLAY",NULL,NULL,NULL);
            bufr= (BYTE*)GlobalLock(m_Bmp.m_hData);
            tmp= bufr + sizeof(BITMAP);
            memcpy(&bm,bufr,sizeof(BITMAP));
            sz= ((bm.bmWidthBytes * bm.bmHeight) *
                bm.bmPlanes);
            pBitmap->CreateCompatibleBitmap(&dc,bm.bmWidth,
                bm.bmHeight);
            pBitmap->SetBitmapBits(sz,tmp);
            GlobalUnlock(m_Bmp.m_hData);
            ret= TRUE;
            }
        }
    return(ret);
}

BOOL dbBmpRecordset::setBitmap(dbBitmap* pBitmap)
{
    BOOL ret= FALSE;
    BYTE* bufr= NULL;// buffer for bitmap struct and the bits
    BYTE* tmp= NULL; // pointer to the start of the bits
    BITMAP bm;
    int sz= NULL;

    if(IsOpen())
        {
        if(pBitmap && pBitmap->m_hObject)
            {
            // get bitmap info
```

```
        pBitmap->GetObject(sizeof(BITMAP),&bm);

        // calculate buffer needed for bitmap bits
        sz= ((bm.bmWidthBytes * bm.bmHeight) * bm.bmPlanes);

        // allocate buffer for bitmap struct AND the bits
        bufr= new BYTE[sz + sizeof(BITMAP) + 1];
        memset(bufr,'\0',sz + sizeof(BITMAP) + 1);

        //  locate start of bits after the bitmap struct
        tmp= bufr + sizeof(BITMAP);

        //  copy the bitmap struct and bits
        memcpy(bufr,&bm,sizeof(BITMAP));
        pBitmap->GetBitmapBits(sz,tmp);

        //  get rid of previous bitmap, if needed
        if(m_Bmp.m_hData)
            GlobalFree(m_Bmp.m_hData);

        //  allocate the bitmap space
        m_Bmp.m_hData= GlobalAlloc(GHND,sz
            +sizeof(BITMAP)+1);
        tmp= (BYTE*)GlobalLock(m_Bmp.m_hData);

        //  copy the bitmap into the long binary field
        memcpy(tmp,bufr,sz + sizeof(BITMAP));
        GlobalUnlock(m_Bmp.m_hData);

        //  now, remember how big the bitmap is *
        m_Bmp.m_dwDataLength= sz + sizeof(BITMAP);

        //  required to manually indacte this field needs
        //  to be stored in the database since it changed
        SetFieldDirty(&(m_Bmp));
        SetFieldNull(&(m_Bmp),FALSE);

        if(bufr)
            delete[] bufr;
        ret= TRUE;
        }
    }
    return(ret);
}


CString dbBmpRecordset::GetDefaultConnect()
{    return "ODBC;DSN=BitmapDB;";    }

CString dbBmpRecordset::GetDefaultSQL()
{    return "BITMAPS";    }

void dbBmpRecordset::DoFieldExchange(CFieldExchange* pFX)
{
```

```
    //{{AFX_FIELD_MAP(dbBmpRecordset)
    pFX->SetFieldType(CFieldExchange::outputColumn);
    RFX_Int(pFX, "ID", m_ID);
    RFX_Text(pFX, "Descr", m_Descr);
    RFX_LongBinary(pFX, "Bmp", m_Bmp);
    //}}AFX_FIELD_MAP
}
//End of File
```

Listing 3: db_bmp.h—Definition of dbBitmap

```
#ifndef __AFXWIN_H__
    #error include 'stdafx.h' before this file for PCH
#endif
#include "resource.h"       // main symbols

class CBmpApp : public CWinApp
{
public:
    CBmpApp();

// Overrides
    virtual BOOL InitInstance();

// Implementation

    //{{AFX_MSG(CBmpApp)
    afx_msg void OnAppAbout();
    // NOTE - the ClassWizard will add and remove member
    // functions here. DO NOT EDIT what you see in these
    // blocks of generated code !
    //}}AFX_MSG
    DECLARE_MESSAGE_MAP()
};
/* End of File */
```

Listing 4: db_bmp.cpp—Implementation of dbBitmap

```
#include "stdafx.h"
#include "db_bmp.h"

#include "bmpfrm.h"
#include "bmpdoc.h"
#include "bmpvw.h"

#ifdef _DEBUG
#undef THIS_FILE
static char BASED_CODE THIS_FILE[] = __FILE__;
#endif

///////////////
// CBmpApp
BEGIN_MESSAGE_MAP(CBmpApp, CWinApp)
```

```
    //{{AFX_MSG_MAP(CBmpApp)
    ON_COMMAND(ID_APP_ABOUT, OnAppAbout)
    // NOTE - the ClassWizard will add and remove mapping
    // macros here. DO NOT EDIT what you see in these blocks
    // of generated code!
    //}}AFX_MSG_MAP
    // Standard file based document commands
    ON_COMMAND(ID_FILE_NEW, CWinApp::OnFileNew)
    ON_COMMAND(ID_FILE_OPEN, CWinApp::OnFileOpen)
END_MESSAGE_MAP()

// CBmpApp construction
CBmpApp::CBmpApp()
{    // TODO: add construction code here,
}

// The one and only CBmpApp object
CBmpApp NEAR theApp;


// CBmpApp initialization
BOOL CBmpApp::InitInstance()
{
// Standard initialization
// If you are not using these features and wish to reduce
// the size of your final executable, you should remove from
// the following the specific initialization routines you do
// not need.

    SetDialogBkColor();   // Set dlg background to gray
    LoadStdProfileSettings(); // Load standard INI options

    // Register the application's document templates.
    CSingleDocTemplate* pDocTemplate;
    pDocTemplate = new CSingleDocTemplate(
        IDR_MAINFRAME,
        RUNTIME_CLASS(CBmpDoc),
        RUNTIME_CLASS(CBmpFrm),     // main SDI frame window
        RUNTIME_CLASS(CBmpView));
    AddDocTemplate(pDocTemplate);

    // create a new (empty) document
    OnFileNew();

    if (m_lpCmdLine[0] != '\0')
    {
        // TODO: add command line processing here
    }
    return TRUE;
}

// CAboutDlg dialog used for App About
class CAboutDlg : public CDialog
{
```

```
public:
    CAboutDlg();

// Dialog Data
    //{{AFX_DATA(CAboutDlg)
    enum { IDD = IDD_ABOUTBOX };
    //}}AFX_DATA

// Implementation
protected:
    virtual void DoDataExchange(CDataExchange* pDX);
    //{{AFX_MSG(CAboutDlg)
        // No message handlers
    //}}AFX_MSG
    DECLARE_MESSAGE_MAP()
};

CAboutDlg::CAboutDlg() : CDialog(CAboutDlg::IDD)
{
    //{{AFX_DATA_INIT(CAboutDlg)
    //}}AFX_DATA_INIT
}

void CAboutDlg::DoDataExchange(CDataExchange* pDX)
{
    CDialog::DoDataExchange(pDX);
    //{{AFX_DATA_MAP(CAboutDlg)
    //}}AFX_DATA_MAP
}

BEGIN_MESSAGE_MAP(CAboutDlg, CDialog)
    //{{AFX_MSG_MAP(CAboutDlg)
        // No message handlers
    //}}AFX_MSG_MAP
END_MESSAGE_MAP()

// App command to run the dialog
void CBmpApp::OnAppAbout()
{
    CAboutDlg aboutDlg;
    aboutDlg.DoModal();
}

///////////////////
// CBmpApp commands
//End of File
```

Indexed Text Retrieval

Robert Krten

With the glut of inexpensive storage devices (disk storage now costs as little as $0.25/MB) and the availability of large bodies of free (or inexpensive) data (telephone directories, Internet documents, FAQs, and the like), getting data onto local storage and indexing it for fast and convenient access has become vitally important. In this article, I'll present an approach to developing a fast, flexible text-retrieval system. While the example I'll develop focuses on a telephone-number database, the design and implementation can easily be adapted to other types of text databases and formats.

My requirements for a telephone-number database were that it:

- Support fairly large amounts of data (549 MB are required for all of Canada, for example).
- Index by phone number in less than one second.
- Index by text keys in several seconds.

Robert is a principal with PARSE Software Devices. He can be contacted at rk@parse.com.
Reprinted courtesy of Dr. Dobb's Journal.

I also wanted the search criteria for the database to be as flexible as possible; for instance, it had to be able to "find all hospitals in Toronto" or "find all the Smiths on Sunset Boulevard." Disk space was not a consideration, because of the low price per megabyte.

I wanted the database to index in less than one second because I subscribe to the phone company's caller-ID service, which delivers the phone numbers of incoming calls between the first and second ring. I wanted to get associated information off my hard disk quickly—before the second ring. This turned out to be simple. In a classic database, the telephone number would serve as the key into the database and would perhaps be hashed, and then looked up. In my database, the telephone number represents a pathname. I can open the file specified by the pathname and do a binary search on it. UNIX file systems are not terribly efficient at searching through thousands of filenames to find the file that you want to open, so I implemented a "digit-tree" file structure.

Digit Tree

In a digit-tree structure, a root directory contains the first digit of the phone number ("6" for "613", for example). Each directory has subdirectories named after the subsequent digits in the phone number. For example, "6135141212" would be stored in a data file called */databaseRoot/6/1/3/5/1/4*, where the last *4* is not a directory, but a file containing all of the *613514* numbers, sorted by the last four digits of the phone number (referred to as the "station code"). Example 1 illustrates what the *4* file might contain.

The advantages of this organization are numerous. First, the file system has to open only a few directory levels (a reasonably quick operation) and search through just one small file. My experience with the telephone directory for Ontario, for instance, indicates that office codes (the "514" in the previous example) are typically about half full—approximately 5000 records. Secondly, a fair amount of data compression is built into this system. Since the individual files are stored in a hierarchical structure, the area code and office-code information are implied by the file pathname itself, and do not have to be repeated as data within the file.

The other advantage is that the 613514 entry is still a small, flat ASCII text file—I can edit it without a specialized (and substantially more limited) database editing utility.

Of course, if you wanted to squeeze some data space out of this scheme, the station code—instead of being represented in 4-character ASCII followed by a space—could be squeezed into just 14 bits (say, two bytes for ease, saving three bytes).

So far, this isn't rocket science. Converting your existing telephone-number database into that particular organization is left as an exercise to the reader—I used a small C program that took a few hours to write and several to run. In fact, strictly speaking, you can use most of the other ideas in this article without reorganizing the database.

Search by Text

To index text keys in several seconds using the scheme described so far, the database is split out by area code and office code over a large number of subdirectories and files (I have 8221 files in my database at the time of writing!). Obviously, it isn't practical to open every file looking for a record that matches a bunch of keys.

Furthermore, not all telephone records have the same data in the same order. As I accumulated telephone-directory information, I merged from many different databases (Canadian White Pages CD-ROM, Ottawa/Hull Pay Phone database, private databases of acquaintances, and the like), each with its own format. (The example for 613514 is typical.) This precluded using the traditional database-design trick of creating last-name, first-name, and street-name indexes.

In fact, I had only two pieces of data that made any sense across all of the different formats: a telephone directory number (DN) and some descriptive text. Since the descriptive text is not "tagged" (as firstname, lastname, address, and so on), it all has to be considered during a keyword search. This means that every word in the database has to be indexed—the premise for the "indexed text retrieval" (ITR) program I present in this article.

Indexed Text Retrieval

By indexing every word, I can search on the logical AND/OR combination of any words I choose. For example, to find all of the hospitals in Ottawa, I just type *itr hospital ottawa*, where *itr* is the name of the ITR program, and *hospital* and *ottawa* are text keywords. The ITR program will print out all phone-number records that match the two keywords. (Note that this version of ITR is case insensitive.)

Implementation of ITR requires two separate programs—an indexing program and a lookup program. Listing One is the ITR.H file for the ITR program, while Listing Two is the main ITR retrieval program, ITR.C. Other relevant files (the ITR Indexer, a common library, and a makefile) are available electronically on the diskette.

Indexing every word involves opening each input file, reading each line (station code and text), and parsing out the words. In my implementation, I skip anything that is not "A" through "Z". Therefore, for each word, I have the following information: filename (in this case, the area code and office code), position (in this case, the station code), and the word itself. I don't care about the word's relative position on the line—I just want it associated with a given DN. Then when I specify the search keys, I don't have to specify them in any particular order; "ottawa hospital" is equivalent to "hospital ottawa."

Managing this amount of data is in itself a challenge since this index is quite large.

Filename	Size (Bytes)	Records
w/e/k.db	36	9
w/e/l/m.db	28	7
w/e/l/e.db	32	8
w/e/l/b.db	1060	265
w/e/l/c.db	2580	645
w/e/l/d/a.db	36	9

Table 1: ***Sample list of files.***

```
1212  Weather Number, 24 hours / day, Ottawa Valley
1213  Liz and Brian's Pizza House, 2666 Temp Street, Ottawa
1443  Pay Phone, 55 Queensway Offramp
```

Example 1: ***Contents of a typical digit-tree file.***

Level	Maximum	Actual	Percentage
1	26	26	100.00
2	676	462	63.02
3	17 576	5 730	32.60
4	456 976	23 949	5.24
5	11 881 376	32 314	<0.01

Table 2: ***Theoretical maximum number of files versus number actually observed in sample database. Consuming 141.2 MB of index for the 549-MB database.***

The Alpha Tree

After the digit-tree approach succeeded, I decided to experiment with an alpha tree. Using this scheme to find the keys for "ottawa," I simply open the file "o/t/t/a/w/a.db" and find all of the keys. The keys are directly translatable into the telephone-database record. To preserve disk space, I had to make some decisions about the extent of the alpha tree. I first chose a maximum depth of five levels. Depending upon the data that you wish to index, this restriction may be drastically altered to suit your requirements.

To generate the index, I implemented a "bucket-sort" algorithm that works like this: During analysis, I take each DN and word and generate a 10-byte entry consisting of six bytes from the word (null padded) and four bytes representing the DN. Then, I append this entry to the file with the same name as the first character of the word. For example, the word "weather" is stripped to just five characters ("weath"), and, along with the key (6135141212), appended to a file called "w.1". The next word, "Number," is also stripped to five characters ("numbe"), and along with the same key, is appended to a file called "n.1".

Once all words in all files are processed, each ".1" file is opened and analyzed. If the number of records in the file warrants splitting it up (this is a tunable parameter in the source), a subdirectory is created and the process repeats, using the next character of the word as the basis for the filename. For example, when the "w.1" file is analyzed, the word "weath" is written to "w/e.1". This process continues until either five levels of directory structure have been generated, or the ".1" file is small enough not to split. Finally, when all of the files are split, the partial word is stripped out of the files since it is no longer required, making each record contain only the 4-byte (telephone number) key.

The final result is an alpha-tree structure on disk with files consisting of indexes representing phone numbers. This is similar to a classical hash function, except that the length of the hash is flexible, depending upon the number of entries. Table 1, which lists the files I have on my disk, shows that not as many words start with "WEK" as with "WELC". Interestingly, as the number of levels increases, so does the theoretical number of files. Table 2 summarizes the theoretical maximum number of files and the number actually contained in my database.

Retrieval Software

To access the stored information, the retriever takes the keywords passed on the command line and finds matching database records. If only one keyword is specified, the retriever opens the associated keyword file; for example, if the keyword is "welcome," the retriever opens "w/e/l/c.db". Then, for each entry in the keyword file, the retriever opens the corresponding database file, performing secondary matching on the database records as they go by. Any records that fully match are printed.

The reason for a secondary match is that ".db" files are unique only as far as their filenames go. For example, the w/e/l/c.db file contains keys for all words that *start* with "welc": "welcome," "welch," and the like.

In the case of two or more keywords, the retriever opens all specified keyword files and finds keys that are the same in all of them. (Since the key files are sorted by key, this is relatively simple.) Once keys are found that are the same in all files, the telephone-database file is opened and a secondary match is performed to check that the keywords are all present in the database entry.

The current version of the retriever (see Listing Two) provides only an AND function—all keywords listed on the command line must match for the record to be printed. It is simple to add an OR capability and partial-key matching.

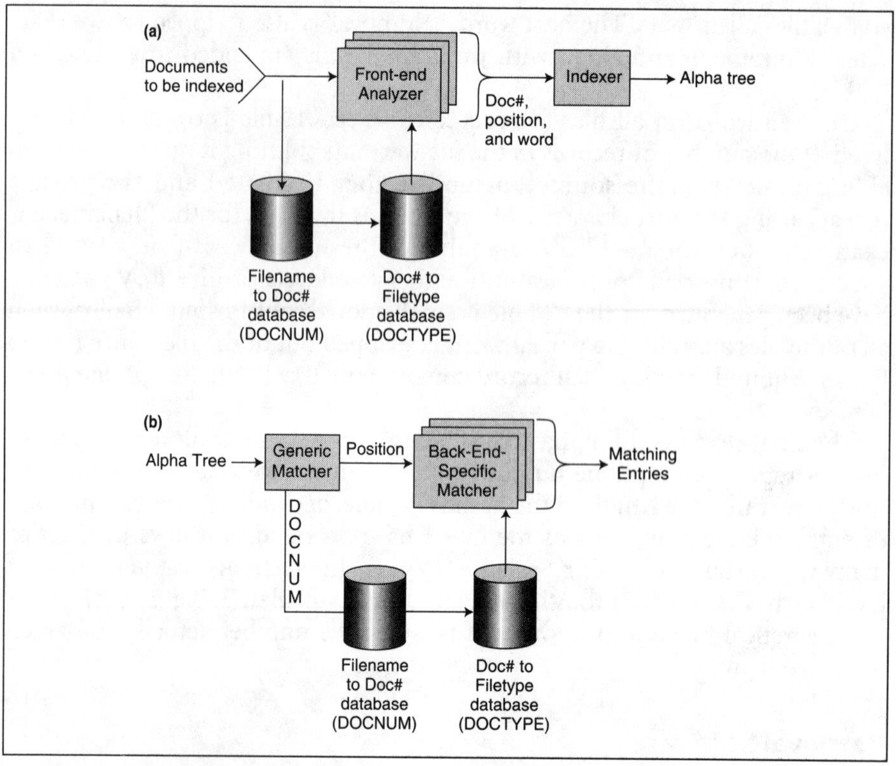

Figure 1: *Implementing an ITR program. (a) INDEXER; (b) RETRIEVER.*

Extending the ITR Concept

How can you extend this system to usefully index arbitrary bodies of text? Start by revisiting the indexer, which generates alpha-tree entries that contained the index. The index consists of a complete telephone number. You interpret the telephone number in two parts; together, the area code and office code make up the "filename," and the station code (the last four digits) is the "record position" within the specified filename.

By revising the indexer to generate 8-byte indexes—four bytes for the filename (as a file ID number, DOCNUM) and four for the word position within that file—arbitrary text can be indexed. In fact, the sample telephone-database indexer is a subset of this approach.

As an aside, you can't really store a complete telephone number into four bytes. I "cheated" by creating a table of area-code and office-code pairs, then stored a six-digit index in this table. For instance, my database has 8221 area-code/office-code pairs, which means that the index ranges from 0000010000 through to 0082219999—well within the range of four bytes. Some string manipulation is then performed on the decimal ASCII representation of the four bytes, and the area-code/office-code pair and station ID are split out or merged in, depending upon the operation being performed.

The interpretation of the 4-byte file position is left up to you. For certain types of database searches, the four bytes might represent the word's byte offset from the start of the file. For other types, it may represent the relative word number in the file. In the telephone-database example, it represents the record number.

Figure 1 illustrates a flexible approach to implementing an ITR program. In this scheme, any documents being added to the ITR database are assigned a document number in the DOCNUM database. This allows an association to be made between the filename (which can be arbitrarily long and complex; hypertext links, for example) and a 4-byte document number to be established.

Next, another database is established that allows the association between the document number and a document type (DOCTYPE). The document type is used by the front-end analysis scheme to choose an appropriate analyzer, and by the back-end matching scheme to choose a corresponding matcher.

To index a file once the DOCNUM and DOCTYPE database entries have been created, every word within the file is processed by the appropriate front-end analyzer; the document number, word position, and word itself are sent to the indexer. The indexer creates/updates the alpha-tree based upon the word, adding the document number and word position at the appropriate place.

To retrieve a document, a generic matcher is passed the list of keywords being searched for, and finds them in the alpha tree. Every time the generic matcher finds a match (based upon the alpha-tree information), it calls the specific matcher for that file type (from the DOCTYPE database) to verify the match. If the match is verified, the appropriate information is printed. Again, depending upon the exact requirements, there may be no need for a back-end matcher; for example, if the alpha-tree information is complete, rather than partial.

Much of the system's flexibility comes into play in the DOCTYPE database and analyzer and matcher. The analyzer and matcher operate as a pair, so it is entirely up to them to interpret the word position returned from the generic matcher. As an example, the DOCTYPE could indicate a PostScript, spreadsheet, word processor, or other type of arbitrary file or document.

Listing One

```
/* itr.h
 * QNX 4
 * (C) Copyright 1993 by Robert Krten, all rights reserved.
 * This module contains the manifest constants and associated declarations
 * for the "ITR" program.
*/

/* manifest constants */

#define MaxDBLineLen        256 /* maximum length of database line */
#define NumKeys             10
#define KeyCacheSize        1024
#define MaxKeyWordLength    64
#define MaxFilenameLength   256
```

```
/* structure definitions */
typedef struct
{
    char    keyword [MaxKeyWordLength];
    char    fname [256];
    FILE    *fp;
    long    val;
    long    *cache;
    int     cachePtr;
    int     maxcache;
}   Key;

/* prototypes */
void        init (void);
void        ftrSearch (void);
void        findNextKey (int);
void        printKey (int);
void        printMatch (int);
void        initKeys (void);
int         databaseMatch (char *, char *);
```

Listing Two

```
/* main.c - QNX 4, main.c shell version 0.004
 * (C) Copyright 1995 by Robert Krten, all rights reserved.
 * This module represents the main module for the itr retriever.
 * This program will retrieve text based on a full-text retrieval database.
*/

#include <stdio.h>
#include <stdlib.h>
#include <string.h>
#include <unistd.h>
#include <time.h>
#include <ctype.h>

#include "itr.h"
#include "lib.h"

char    *progname = "itr";

char    phoneDB [MaxFilenameLength];      /* database filename roots */
char    root [MaxFilenameLength];         /* base of itr database */
char    npanxx [MaxFilenameLength];       /* base of document # xlat */
char    *translation;                     /* allocated by read_translation */
int     numtrans;                         /* number of above */
int     longerThanIndex [NumKeys];        /* 1 if strlen (searchWord) > 5 */
long    topKey;                           /* highest of any */
long    maxKey;                           /* largest valid key */
int     numSearch;
Key     keys [NumKeys];
```

```
/* the main key structure */

main (argc, argv)
int      argc;
char    **argv;
{
    optproc (argc, argv);   /* get keys from command line */
    init ();                /* initialize search engine */
    itrSearch ();           /* search engine */
}
void
optproc (argc, argv)
int     argc;
char    **argv;
{
    int     i;
    numSearch = 0;
    for (i = 1; i < argc; i++) {
        if (numSearch >= NumKeys - 1) {
              fprintf (stderr, "%s:  Too many search keys, limit is %d\n",
                                               progname, NumKeys);
              exit (1);
        }
        strcpy (keys [numSearch++].keyword, argv [i]);
    }
}
void
init ()
{
    char    *p;
    if ((p = getenv ("PHONEDB")) != NULL) {
    strcpy (phoneDB, p);
    } else {
        strcpy (phoneDB, "/data/telecom/phoneDB");
    }
    if (phoneDB [strlen (phoneDB) - 1] != '/') {
        strcat (phoneDB, "/");
    }
    sprintf (root, "%s1", phoneDB);
        sprintf (npanxx, "%s/.npanxx", root);
    read_translation (npanxx);          /* fetch the translation table */
    maxKey = numtrans * 10000 + 9999;   /* maximum key value */
}
/* prepareSearchFname - generate alpha-tree pathnames corresponding to each
 * keyword specified.
*/
void
prepareSearchFnames ()
{
    int     i;
    int     l;
    FILE    *fp;
    char    shortFnames [NumKeys][11];  /* /a/b/c/d/e\0 */
```

```
    for (i = 0; i < numSearch; i++) {
        /* generate flag array */
        longerThanIndex [i] = strlen (keys [i].keyword) > 5;
        /* trim search key */
        for (l = 0; l < 5; l++) {
           shortFnames [i][l * 2 + 0] = '/';
           shortFnames [i][l * 2 + 1] = tolower (keys [i].keyword [l]);
        }
        shortFnames [i][10] = 0;    /* terminate preventively */
        /* for short strings, the \0 that got stuck into shortFnames is
         * almost doing its job-there will be a trailing '/' which we
         * kill off here
        */
        if (shortFnames [i][strlen (shortFnames [i]) - 1] == '/') {
            shortFnames [i][strlen (shortFnames [i]) - 1] = 0;
        }
        /* now, see which ones are valid. If not valid, trim off two characters
         * at the end and try again. For short filenames, we (uselessly) trim
         * off characters after the \0 - this all comes out in the wash.
        */
        for (l = 4; l >= 0; l-) {
            sprintf (keys [i].fname, "%s%s.db", root, shortFnames [i]);
            if ((fp = fopen (keys [i].fname, "r")) != NULL) {
                break;
            }
            shortFnames [i][l * 2] = 0; /* kill off part of name */
    }
    if (fp != NULL) {
        fclose (fp);
    } else {
        fprintf (stderr, "%s:  couldn't find database for
                             keyword %s!!!\n", progname, keys [i].keyword);
        exit (1);
    }
  }
}
/* itrSearch - The search engine itself.
 * We change the keywords that we are searching for into actual alpha-tree
 * filenames (via preparseSearchFnames).  Then, we open all searchkey files,
 * and try to find keys that match.
*/
void
itrSearch ()
{
    int     i;
    int     change;
    int     allEqual;

    /* translate search strings into valid filenames */

    if (isdigit (keys [0].keyword [0])) {  /* kludge - if it's a number */
             if (strlen (keys [0].keyword) != 10) {
               fprintf (stderr, "%s: reverse number lookup requires a
                                              10 digit DN!\n", progname);
```

```
            exit (1);
        }
        reverseLookup (keys [0].keyword);
        return;                                         /* done */
    }
    prepareSearchFnames ();
    initKeys ();

/* initialize variables for search */

    for (i = 0; i < numSearch; i++) {
            keys [i].val = 0;
    }
    topKey = 0;                 /* init, findNextKey uses it */

    /* now the real search algorithm begins. Initialize by searching first
     * file, and assigning to 'topKey'
     */
    findNextKey (0);          /* find next (ie:  first) key for string zero */
    topKey = keys [0].val;
    while (topKey != -1) {  /* until EOF */

      /* advance all keys that are below topKey, until they are either at
       * topKey, or above. If a key goes above topKey, reassign topKey and
       * continue. If a key is equal, skip until all keys are equal, or
       * topKey has been adjusted. If all keys are equal, emit a match, and
       * advance any key. Ensure that key has in fact advanced!
       */
      change = 1;
      while (change) {
          change = 0;
          for (i = 0; i < numSearch; i++) {
            while (keys [i].val < topKey && keys [i].val != -1) {
                findNextKey (i);
                if (keys [i].val > topKey) {
                    topKey = keys [i].val;
                    change = 1;
                }
            }
            if (keys [i].val == -1) {
                return;
            }
        }
    }
    /* since there is no more change, ensure all keys are equal */
    allEqual = 1;
    for (i = 0; i < numSearch - 1; i++) {
        if (keys [i].val != keys [i + 1].val) {
            allEqual = 0;
        }
    }
    if (!allEqual) {
        return;           /* Couldn't find a match */
    }
```

```
        printMatch (keys [0].val);    /* validate and then show matches */
        while (keys [0].val == topKey) {
          findNextKey (0);    /* advance to next search */
        }
        topKey = keys [0].val;
    }
}
/* reverseLookup - prints database entry associated with the passed DN */
void
reverseLookup (dn)
char *dn;
{
     char    obuf [256];
     if (databaseMatch (dn, obuf)) {
             printf ("%s:  %s\n", dn, obuf);
        } else {
             printf ("No match\n");
    }
}
void
initKeys ()
{
    int     i;
    for (i = 0; i < numSearch; i++) {
        if ((keys [i].fp = fopen (keys [i].fname, "r")) == NULL) {
            fprintf (stderr, "%s:  couldn't open %s for r\n",
                     progname, keys [i].fname);
            exit (1);
        }
        if ((keys [i].cache = malloc (sizeof (long) *
                                            KeyCacheSize)) == NULL) {
                fprintf (stderr, "%s:  couldn't allocate a cache of %d
                            bytes!\n", progname, sizeof (long) * KeyCacheSize);
            exit (1);
        }
        keys [i].maxcache = fread (keys [i].cache, sizeof (long),
                           KeyCacheSize, keys [i].fp);
        if (keys [i].maxcache < KeyCacheSize) {
                fclose (keys [i].fp); /* close it, we've read it all */
                        keys [i].fp = NULL;  /* indicate closed */
                }
                keys [i].cachePtr = 0;          /* current position for read */
         }
}
/* findNextKey - fetches next key that is greater than "topKey" for the given
 * keyword number, and handles the cache aspects too.
*/
void
findNextKey (k)
int k;              /* search string number */
{
     /* could be replaced with binary search for even greater speed */
     do {
            if (keys [k].cachePtr < keys [k].maxcache) {
```

```
                keys [k].val = keys [k].cache [keys [k].cachePtr++];
                                                    /* "read" value */
        } else {        /* exceeded cache */
              if (keys [k].fp == NULL) {  /* no more to read, done */
                  keys [k].val = -1; /* set EOF */
              } else {
                keys [k].maxcache = fread (keys [k].cache, sizeof (long),
                                         KeyCacheSize, keys [k].fp);
                    if (keys [k].maxcache < KeyCacheSize) {
                          fclose (keys [k].fp);
                          keys [k].fp = NULL;
                    }
                    keys [k].val = keys [k].cache [0];
                    keys [k].cachePtr = 1;
                }
            }
    } while ((keys [k].val < topKey) && (keys [k].val != -1));
}
/* printMatch - fetches matching record, and performs secondary matching
 *  validation on it.  Due to the algorithm used in the ITR program,
 *  it is possible that a "false match" will be generated (see article).
 *  The procedure ensures that no false matches are printed.
*/
void
printMatch (key)
int        key;
{
   char    number [256];           /* translated key -> number */
   char    result [256];           /* database record fetched */
   char    buf [16];               /* temp, key -> ASCII xlat */
   int         npanxx;             /* temp, NPA/NXX from key */
   int         station;            /* temp, station code from key */
   int         matching [NumKeys]; /* matching key matrix 1==match */
   char    word [256];             /* word buffer for 2ndary matches */
   char    *ptr;                   /* buffer pointer for fetching words */
   int         i;
   if (key == -1) {
            printf ("<EOF>\n");
   } else if (key > maxKey) {
            printf ("<INVALID %010ld>\n", key);
   } else {
           sprintf (buf, "%010ld", key);
           station = atoi (buf + 6);
           buf [6] = 0;
           npanxx = atoi (buf);
           sprintf (number, "%6.6s%04d", &translation [npanxx * 7], station);
           /* fetch complete database record into 'result' */
           if (databaseMatch (number, result)) {
                 /* now check 2ndary matches on all keys */
                 for (i = 0; i < numSearch; i++) {
                        matching [i] = 0;          /* initially, no matches */
                 }
                 ptr = result;
                 while (getWordLC (&ptr, word)) {
```

```
                    for (i = 0; i < numSearch; i++) {
                           if (!strcmpi (word, keys [i].keyword)) {
                                        matching [i] = 1;
                           }
                    }
             }
             /* see if all matched 2ndary search */
             for (i = 0; i < numSearch; i++) {
                    if (!matching [i]) {
                           break;
                    }
             }
             if (i == numSearch) {
                printf ("%s %s\n", number, result); /* all matched, print */
             } /* else didn't match *all* keys! */
    } else {
       /* internal bug, couldn't find key in database */
             printf ("Can't match %s in database!!!\n", number);
       }
    }
}
static        char tmpbuf [MaxDBLineLen];
/* databaseMatch - uses binary search with variable length lines to find
 * the number in the text database.
*/

int
databaseMatch (number, result)
char    *number;                                  /* international DN */
char    *result;                                  /* looked-up name, or \0 */
{
    FILE    *fpr;                             /* db open for read */
    char    *ptr;
    int     len;
    long    top, bot;                         /* binary search values */
    long    mid;
    int     sts;
    createDigitTreeName (number, tmpbuf);
    if ((fpr = fopen (tmpbuf, "r")) == NULL) {
             return (0);
    }
    len = strlen (number);          /* how big is the number? */

    bot = 0;                        /* start of the file */
    fseek (fpr, 0L, 2);             /* get to end */
    top = ftell (fpr);              /* limit the search */

    while (top - bot > 512) {       /* while it's worthwhile */
          mid = (top + bot) / 2;
          fseek (fpr, mid, 0);
          fgets (tmpbuf,MaxDBLineLen, fpr); /* skip to end of damaged record */
          mid = ftell (fpr);
          fgets (tmpbuf, MaxDBLineLen, fpr);
          tmpbuf [strlen (tmpbuf) - 1] = 0;
          if (!(sts = strncmp (number + len - 4, tmpbuf, 4))) {
```

```
                ptr = tmpbuf + 4;
                while (*ptr && isspace (*ptr)) {
                        ptr++;
                }
                strcpy (result, ptr);
                fclose (fpr);
                return (1);
        } else {
                if (sts < 0) {
                      top = mid;
                } else {
                      bot = mid;
                }
        }
 }
 fseek (fpr, bot, 0);                    /* rewind to last "bot" position */
 while (!feof (fpr) && fgets (tmpbuf, MaxDBLineLen, fpr) != NULL) {
        tmpbuf [strlen (tmpbuf) - 1] = 0;
        if (!(sts = strncmp (number + len - 4, tmpbuf, 4))) {
              ptr = tmpbuf + 4;
              while (*ptr && isspace (*ptr)) {
                      ptr++;
              }
              strcpy (result, ptr);
              fclose (fpr);
              return (1);
        }
        if (sts < 0) {                  /* exceeded number, must not be there */
              return (0);
        }
  }
  fclose (fpr);
  return (0);
}
/* converts "num" to a digit-tree "path" */
createDigitTreeName (num, path)
char       *num;
char       *path;
{
          int      len;
          char     *ptr;
          *path = 0;
          sprintf (path, "%s/", root);
          ptr = &path [strlen (path)];
          len = strlen (num);
          while (len > 4) {
               *ptr++ = *num++;
               *ptr++ = '/';
               *ptr = 0;
               len—;
          }
         —ptr;
         *ptr = 0;
}
```

Index

A

B

C

G

H

I

J

K

L

M

N

O

P

V

W

X